Creating
Realistic Works of Art
with Barbed Wire

Hairless
Short-haired
Long-haired
Fur
Wool
Wings

by Bernie Jestrabek-Hart

authorHOUSE®

AuthorHouse™
1663 Liberty Drive
Bloomington, IN 47403
www.authorhouse.com
Phone: 1 (800) 839-8640

Published by AuthorHouse 07/26/2018

ISBN: 978-1-5462-4975-7 (sc)
ISBN: 978-1-5462-4974-0 (e)

Print information available on the last page.

TABLE OF CONTENTS

Bernie demonstrating at a show in 2005

I dedicate this book to my two best creations, my sons, Bevan and Trevor Hart. To Bevan, for encouraging me to share my knowledge and for your suggestions in format and editing. To Trevor, thanks for all of your help with editing.

.
In addition, my thanks to my friend, Rosellen Villarreal-Price for proofing and editing.

And to Susan McMonagle, my lifesaver, for the final proofing and editing and lavish praise.

About the Author/Artist

Bernie Jestrabek-Hart is known internationally as an artist who works in metal of all kinds. Barbed wire is her favorite medium.

Bernie has a degree in Art Education and taught art for 6 years before beginning to raise her family. In the fall of 1980, she took a sculpture class at Boise State University which included welded wire and steel sculptures. There she created "Hero"(Picture 1). Following that she bought her oxygen and acetylene welding unit. When seeing a roll of barbed wire she decided to create a bison (Picture 2) from it. She fell in love with the texture and this started her romance with this medium.

The first large commission in barbed wire was for the Idaho First National Bank in Boise, Idaho, currently the US. Bank. It's name "1867" (Picture 6) stands for the year the bank originated.

The first life-size piece was *"Katherine the Great"* (Picture 3) which was later turned into *"Me Llama Llamo"* (Picture 4). The piece that started her career in sculpting was *"Say What Mom?!"* (Picture 5). This is when Bernie turned her sculpting efforts into her full time career. *"Say What Mom?!"* initiated several of the first commissions including *"Mare and Foal"* (Picture 7) for Oregon's High Desert Museum and *"Winning Team (Amber and Clyde)"*(Picture 8).

She has also completed many sculptures in steel, aluminum and stainless steel. However, barbed wire remains her focus. Her hope is that from this book you will also obtain a love for the fantastic medium of barbed wire.

(To see more of Bernie's work see www.sculptures-by-bjh.com)

Photo by Deb Ritch

Picture 1 *"Hero"*
Wire, polished & lacquered
Sacramento, CA

Photo by Duane Garret

Picture 2 *"American Bison"*
Barbed wire, gun metal bluing
Boise, Idaho

Picture 3 *"Katherine the Great"*
with her real-life friends   Barbed wire - rusted

Picture 4 *"Me Llama Llamo"*
Barbed wire - rusted and painted

photo by Deb Ritch

Picture 5 *"Say What, Mom ?!"*
Private collection
Weatherford, Texas
barbed wire, rusted

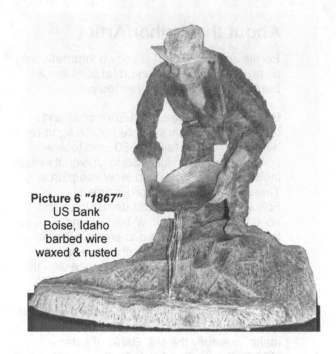

Picture 6 *"1867"*
US Bank
Boise, Idaho
barbed wire
waxed & rusted

Picture 7
The High Desert Museum
Bend, Oregon
"Mare and Foal"
barbed wire, rusted

Picture 8 Hudson Museum
in Parkdale, Oregon
*"Winning Team
(Amber & Clyde)"*
Barbed wire and
sheet steel, painted

v

Before you begin, keep in mind ...

This book will give you an understanding of how I create realistic works with barbed wire. I am not explaining every detail, as I take for granted that you have a good "eye" in order to capture the shape and proportions of what you are creating.

I also take for granted that you know how to weld with Oxygen and Acetylene. I touch briefly on these things, but you will need comprehensive training in these areas if you are a beginner. Be sure to use appropriate safety gear and follow all safety precautions at all times.

I love the barbed wire because of the texture the twisted wire makes. The barbs are really immaterial and often actually get in the way. When this happens I cut or weld them off in that area. When I want it to be smooth I often use the barbs to weld the wire together, thus getting rid of the actual barb, or melt the barbs into the wire along the way. If it is not in a place that needs to be welded, I will often still weld them down so the finished sculpture smooth to the touch. Just to preserve the "romance" of barbed wire, I will leave just a few barbs but keep them in areas that will not be touched.

This is a labor of love, I trust you will enjoy what I am sharing of my art.

-Bernie Jestrabek-Hart

Part I
The Principles of Successful Creation

Chapter 1

Many people have asked me, "How do you make them so real?" or "How did you do this, or that ... ?" This book will try to answer these questions. My goal is to help others find and develop their talents, and discover the pleasure I have received from creating.

There are three equally important principles in the creative process:

1) **Take charge and have faith. Know that you can do the project that you want to do.** Even if you lack some knowledge at this time, you can figure it out. Talk with people who have expertise in the areas in which you have not had experience.

    For example:
    > If you need to weld, take a class or talk to a welder. I am constantly talking with people who know how to weld. Companies that sell the gases and welding supplies are usually very helpful. People who stop by often give good hints. Listen to everyone and pick out the items that help you achieve your goal.

2) **Research, research, research, research, research, research, research, research and research some more:**
    a) How to use the materials
    b) What tools to use
    c) How the subject looks. If the subject is alive, look at the real thing whenever possible. Pictures and videos also help but the real thing is your best model; I cannot stress research enough. If I am creating an elk, I look at elk throughout the process.

3) **Do not be afraid of making a mistake!** Mistakes can teach a great deal and are a natural step in learning. If it is wrong, fix it, change it, work with it until you get it right.

    For example:
    > I created four eagles for the entrances to a business park. I had already created two, and liked their heads. The third one took seven tries to get it correct. I just kept working at it until I was satisfied.

    > When asked "How long does it take?" The answer is "It depends on whether I get it right the first time, second time, or third time!" And so on.

*Especially if you believe your talent is "God-given," you have to know that it is always there for you to develop and use. Take ownership of it. You do not have to wait until "the mood strikes" or until "God flows through you," as many say. (If you believe in God then know that He is always there and so is His gift.) Whether you believe it comes from God or not, when you take ownership of that gift you can gain access to it at any time. Sometimes it will be difficult to figure something out. That is when research and study come into the creation process.

Sometimes it takes time to visualize the way to complete a project. For me, when I figure it out then I am "in the mood." However, I no longer have to wait for such a time. I am able to make it happen. That is what I mean when I say you must "know" and "take charge of" your talent.

I believe that with the above principles as part of your process, You can create anything!

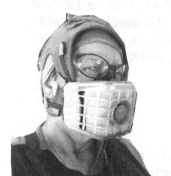

Picture 2.1 Shows one of many choices of fume respirators that fit under the welding hood

Chapter 2
There are many different tools that are used when creating with Barbed Wire. Some are tools I purchase and some I make.

Respirator
It is imperative that you wear a good respirator for fumes (not just dust) because welding fumes are detrimental to your health. Barbed wire, if galvanized, will release zinc in a gaseous form which is deadly if you breath it into your lungs.

Protective Equipment
When welding, it's important to use protective gear, including leather coverings to shield you from sparks. Sometimes I will think, " I only have a couple of minutes of welding so I will not go to the trouble of putting on all the gear." I inevitably get burned.

To the right is a caricature of me created by my older son, Trevor, in all my gear. This shows my leather sleeves, chaps, apron and the helmet for MIG* welding and noise protection when using a grinder or other loud tools.

Be sure to use all the items needed for safety.

Follow the manufacturers' recommendations regarding tool safety. Please be safe so you can enjoy creating.

Picture 2.2 Caricature by Trevor Hart
www.ashlar-online.com

*GMAW or Gas Metal Arc Welding is referred to as MIG welding.

Cutting a Roll of Wire

I use old barbed wire that has never been galvanized when I can find it. The best was made before 1950. It is good quality soft steel and welds easily. The new wire is often made from recycled steel and does not weld easily.

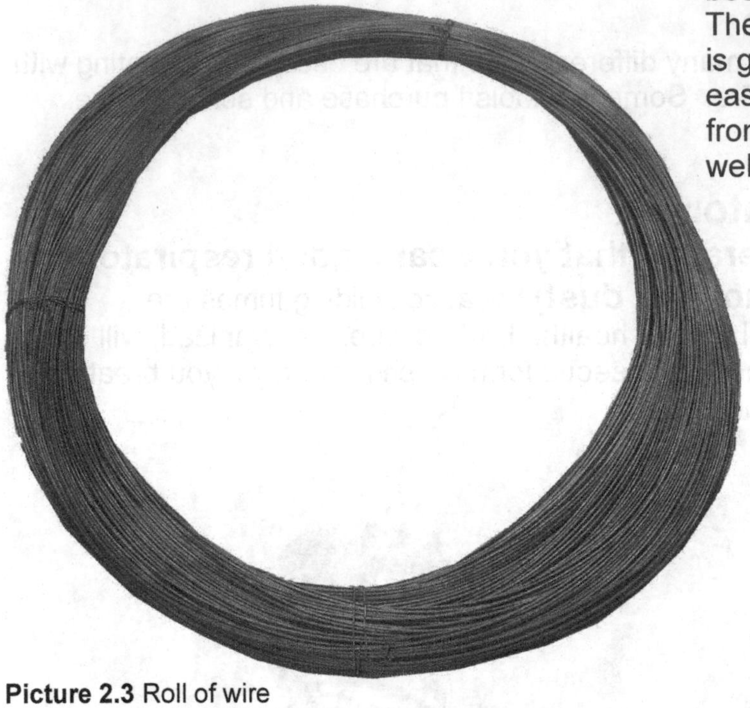

The wire can be cut one piece at a time with wire cutters, or cut faster with a skill saw using a metal cutting blade.

Picture 2.3 Roll of wire

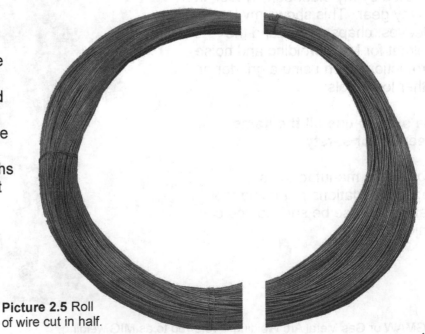

Picture 2.4 Skill saw with metal cutting blade

I cut the roll in half or into thirds, depending on the circumference of the roll. The finished pieces of wire should be 2 to 3 ½ feet in length. I seldom can weld to the end of a wire, which leaves a short piece of wire on the end that cannot be used. Using shorter lengths creates an excess of short pieces of unusable wire. Longer pieces of wire are too hard to maneuver.

Picture 2.5 Roll of wire cut in half.

4

Welding

I will not spend a lot of time discussing welding technique, as that is a course in itself. I will concentrate on the creative process I use for barbed wire sculptures.

The main kind of welding equipment I use for barbed wire is oxygen-acetylene. You can also use MIG (also called Wire Feed) or Stick (ARC) welding equipment.

The reason I prefer oxygen-acetylene welding it that with this type of welding, I can heat the wire to bend it but don't have to weld where I bend it. I get a much better bend and can control the wire when heating it first. With a MIG or stick welder, I cannot heat the wire so it bends easily.

I use the smaller torch, called an "airplane torch" because this torch does not run as hot as the regular large torch. The lighter weight of this smaller torch makes it much easier on my hands, arms and shoulders. With so many working hours holding the torch, I am prone to repetitive injury issues. The lighter torches are much easier for me to use for longer periods of time.

Picture 2.6 allows you to see the relative size of the jeweler's torch, airplane torch and a regular torch; the torches are not shown actual size, but show relative size. I use the airplane torch for barbed wire, and the jeweler's to weld smaller wire.

There are other items involved with welding oxygen-acetylene, including hoses, gauges, gas cylinders, and strikers. Check with your local welding supply store for more complete information.

Look for classes at a community college or ask your local welding supply store where there are classes on welding.

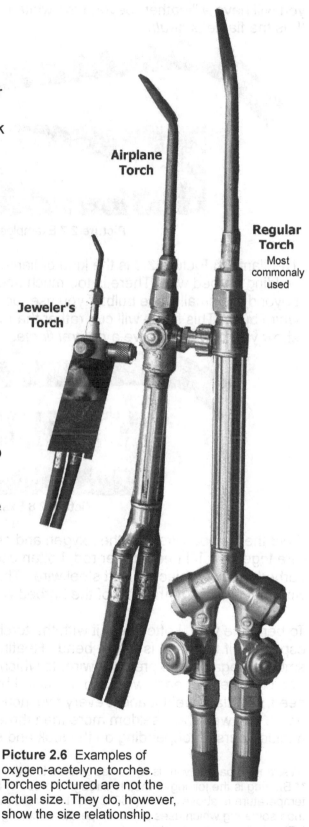

Airplane Torch

Regular Torch Most commonaly used

Jeweler's Torch

Picture 2.6 Examples of oxygen-acetelyne torches. Torches pictured are not the actual size. They do, however, show the size relationship.

In my experience, the best way to weld barbed wire with oxygen-acetylene is with a *neutral flame*. Below is a drawing and photo of a neutral flame. The arrow points to the white well-defined bulb that shows the flame is neutral. If there is too much acetylene, you will have a "feather" beyond the white flame. (See Picture 2.7) You want no *feather*, thus the flame is *neutral*.

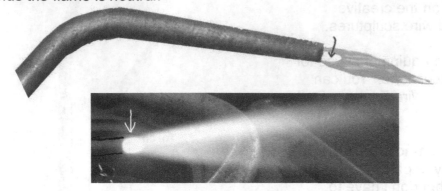

Picture 2.7 Examples of a *neutral flame*

The flame in Picture 2.8 is the kind of flame that is used for brazing**, and not for welding barbed wire. There is too much acetylene, causing the flame to "feather" beyond the small white bulb. If you use too much oxygen, you will have a very small white bulb. This flame will cut, rather than weld well. If you are unsure, have someone show you how to achieve a *neutral flame*.

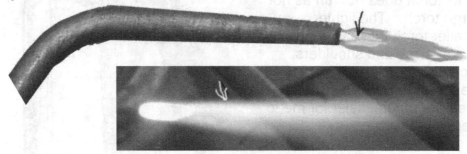

Picture 2.8 Examples of a *"feather"*

Weld the barbed wire with the oxygen and acetylene, using the neutral flame. Melt the wire together. If I need a filler rod, I often use an unwrapped piece from a strand* of barbed wire or a piece of soft steel wire. This steel wire can be any gauge of wire, but wire that is close to the size of the barbed wire that is being used works best.

To bend the wire, I often heat it with the torch to make it softer and easy to bend, especially if the bend is a tight bend. Heating it also helps to keep twisted wire to lie smoothly against the previous wire, to which it will be welded. I weld it with close welds. The closeness of each weld is determined by the way the wire lies and the strength you need. I usually weld it about every two inches, sometimes closer and sometimes further apart. My welds are seldom more than three inches apart. This is something you can decide yourself, depending on the look and strength that you want.

*A strand of barbed wire is two wires twisted together with one containing barbs.
** Brazing is the joining of metals through the use of heat and a filler metal. The filler metal has a melting temperature is above 840°F (450°C) but below the melting pint of the metals being joined. This is different than soldering which uses a low temperature melting point alloy for the filler metal and a soldering gun instead of a welding torch.

6

Other basic tools needed and that can be purchased from a store are hammers, pliers, wire cutters, grinders, wire brushes, and clamps.

Grinders

I usually keep a grinder unit with a wire brush (Picture 2.10) and another unit with a grinding wheel (picture 2.9) available. I typically use both units on the same project, one after the other. Using two units saves time by eliminating the need to change attachments.

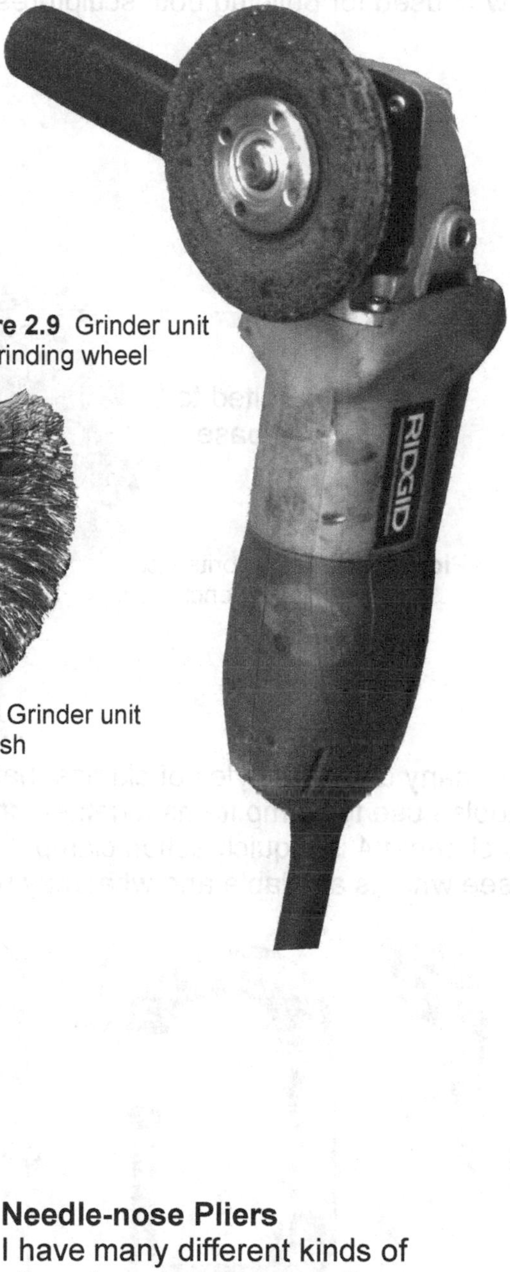

Picture 2.9 Grinder unit with grinding wheel

Picture 2.10 Grinder unit with wire brush

Wire Cutters

I use two different sizes of wire cutters, a small one to cut wire 12-gauge or smaller and a larger cutter that will cut up to 1/4" rod.

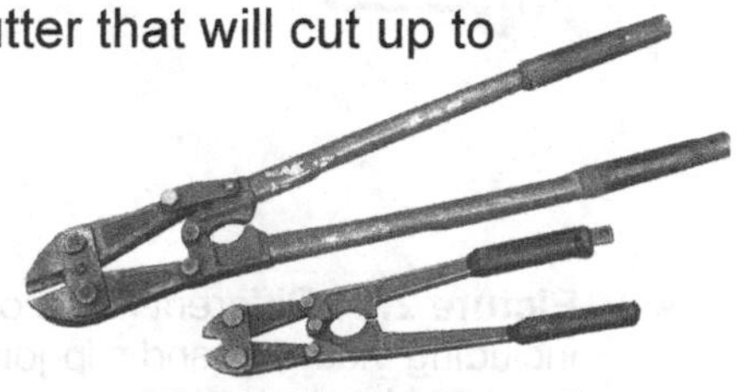

Picture 2.11 Wire cutters

Needle-nose Pliers

I have many different kinds of pliers; however, my favorite are needle-nose pliers. I have several pairs and keep them handy when working. I find that I often drop or misplace one, so I have another ready to use.

Picture 2.12 Needle-nose pliers

7

Vises

There are many types and sizes of vises. The bench vise in Picture 2.13 is one that I often use. It is very handy because it can be adjusted to various positions. This is the vise that was used for building both sculptures shown as "in process" in this book.

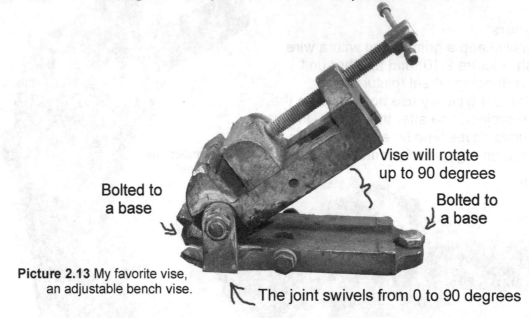

Bolted to a base

Vise will rotate up to 90 degrees

Bolted to a base

The joint swivels from 0 to 90 degrees

Picture 2.13 My favorite vise, an adjustable bench vise.

Clamps

There are many different styles of clamps that can be used. In picture 2.14 there are several tools I use to clamp items together. #1 is a vise grip. #2 shows slip-joint pliers. #3 is a C clamp; #4 is a quick-action clamp. Check with your local hardware or welding store to see what is available and what may work best for you.

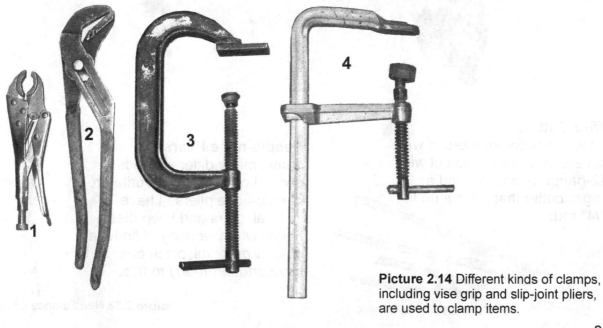

Picture 2.14 Different kinds of clamps, including vise grip and slip-joint pliers, are used to clamp items.

Useful Tools I Created

Hammer

There are many kinds of hammers. Check your local hardware stores for a good selection.

My favorite hammer is one I made from a railroad spike and a piece of pipe, welded together (See Picture 2.15). It is well balanced and it gives me both a round end and a spiked end with which to hammer. I made a second hammer with the spike attached at a 90-degree angle, to give me a different angle on the round and the spike end.

Picture 2.15 My favorite hammer

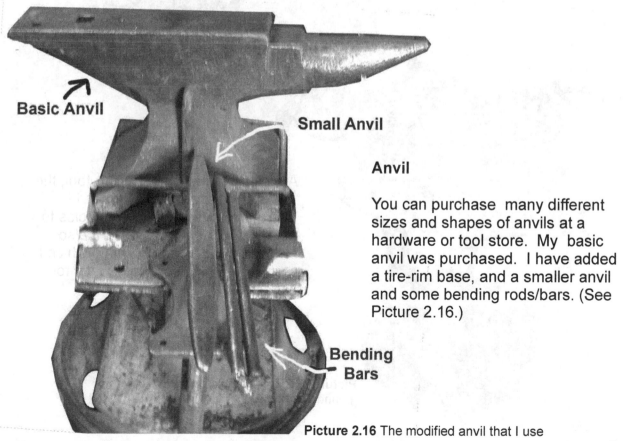

Basic Anvil

Small Anvil

Bending Bars

Anvil

You can purchase many different sizes and shapes of anvils at a hardware or tool store. My basic anvil was purchased. I have added a tire-rim base, and a smaller anvil and some bending rods/bars. (See Picture 2.16.)

Picture 2.16 The modified anvil that I use

9

Bending and Shaping Tools

This shaping tool is made with different sizes of pipe and a disc base.

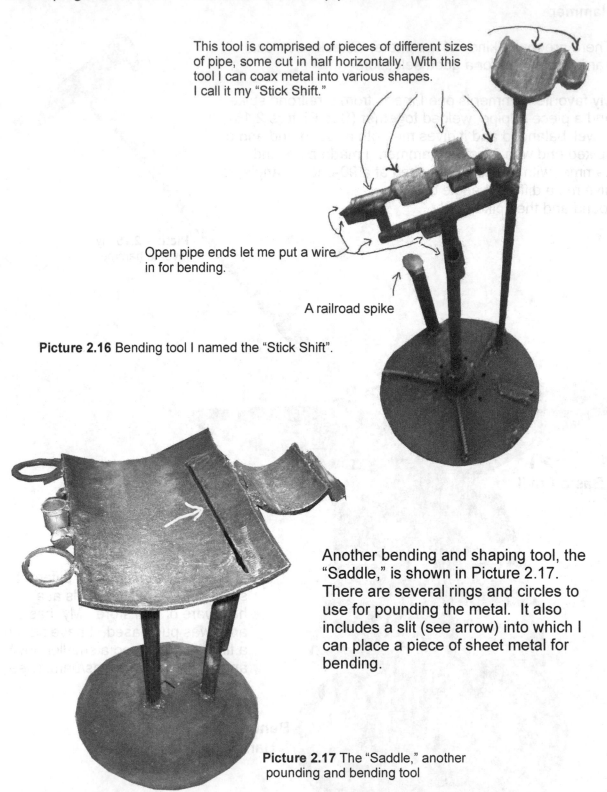

This tool is comprised of pieces of different sizes of pipe, some cut in half horizontally. With this tool I can coax metal into various shapes. I call it my "Stick Shift."

Open pipe ends let me put a wire in for bending.

A railroad spike

Picture 2.16 Bending tool I named the "Stick Shift".

Another bending and shaping tool, the "Saddle," is shown in Picture 2.17. There are several rings and circles to use for pounding the metal. It also includes a slit (see arrow) into which I can place a piece of sheet metal for bending.

Picture 2.17 The "Saddle," another pounding and bending tool

10

More Homemade Bending Tools

There are many instances in which I need either to bend a wire or rod, or beat or bend a section of rod either in or out. I have found that the tools that I show on this page, work well for this purpose.

Picture 2.18 shows several tools that are made from pipe and/or rod. #1 is a long pipe with different-sized pounding shapes at each end. I use this on large sculptures when an area needs to be pounded out after most of the sculpture has been completed. I may have to cut a hole on one side of the sculpture to put this tool through so I can to pound out the other side from the inside. This is a heavy tool and is used a lot like a digging bar; the weight helps me produce a powerful hit.

Tools # 2, 3, 4, and 5 are bending tools of different sizes.

Picture 2.19 shows how tool #1, shown in both Pictures 2.18 and 2.19, can bend a flat piece (see 1b). The piece is inserted into the end to bend. 2, 3, and 4 can bend something the same way. As seen in Picture 2.19, Tool #1 can do the same on the 1b end. It can also bend a rod or wire on either end when I put the wire or rod through the end of the tool.(1a)

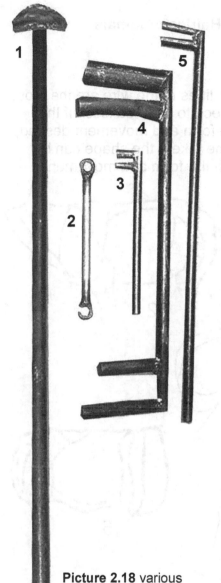

Picture 2.18 various bending and pounding tools

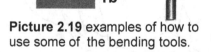

Picture 2.19 examples of how to use some of the bending tools.

Plasma Cutter

I often use a plasma cutter, a machine that uses of air and electricity to cut metal. It cuts metal much faster and cleaner than cutting with a torch. It is very handy for cutting out mistakes. There are many kinds of plasma cutters available, so I will not show or name a specific one. I created for years without a plasma cutter and got along well by cutting with my oxygen-acetelyne cutting-torch. However, since aquiring one, I cannot believe how much I use it and I wonder how I got along without one for so long.

Part III
Techniques for Creating Short-haired and Hairless Animals

Chapter 3 - Lines

When using wire to portray the movement of the piece, the lines of the wire are the most important feature. This is especially true if you want the piece to look realistic. If the shape is correct but the lines of the wire do not go with the form and movement desired, the piece will not look realistic or show motion. By the same token, the shape can be somewhat incorrect, as long as the lines of the wire go with the form and movement. There can be many variations that still look accurate.

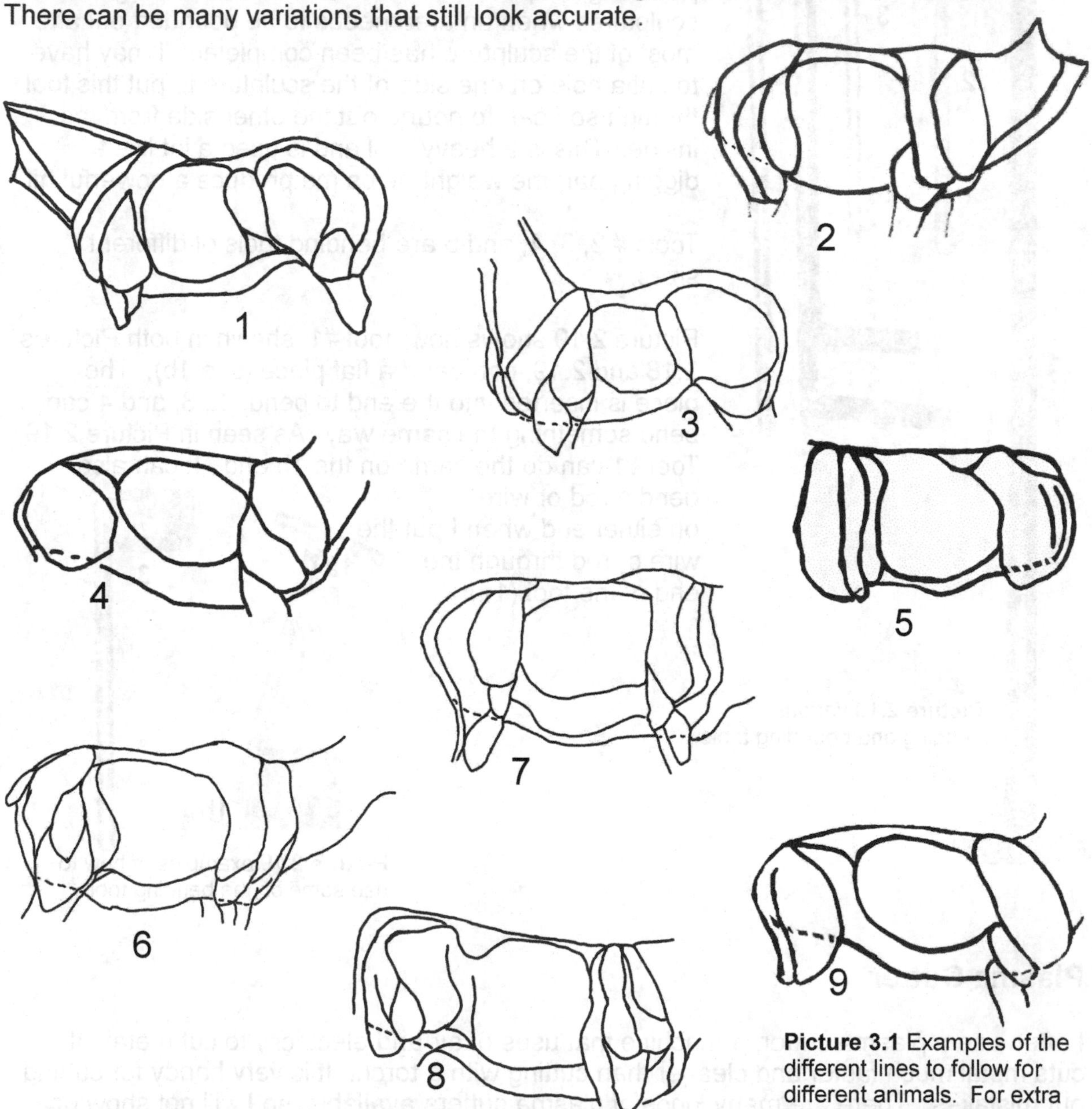

Picture 3.1 Examples of the different lines to follow for different animals. For extra credit, name the animals.

1. Horse 2. Elk 3. Foal 4. Deer 5. Cow 6. Elk 7. Elk 8. Calf 9. Deer

12

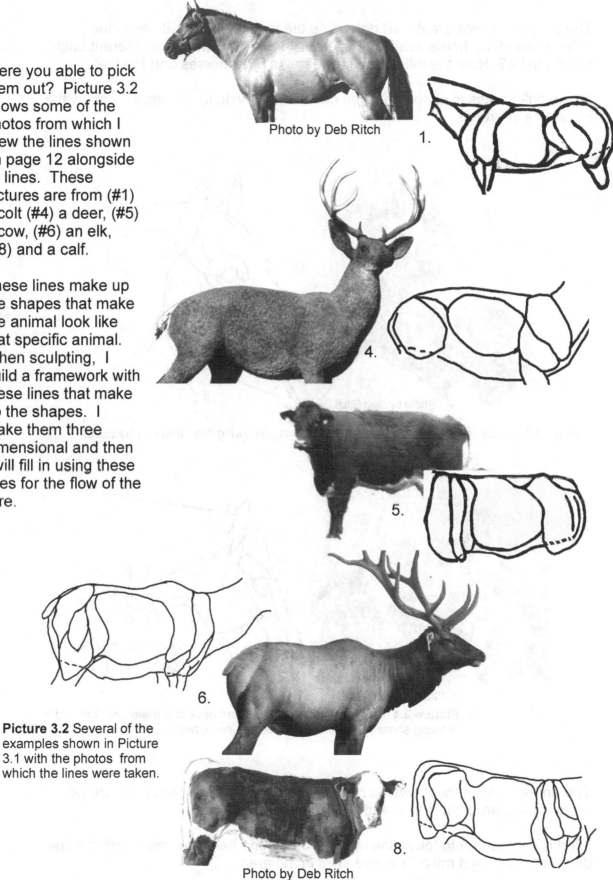

Were you able to pick them out? Picture 3.2 shows some of the photos from which I drew the lines shown on page 12 alongside its lines. These pictures are from (#1) a colt (#4) a deer, (#5) a cow, (#6) an elk, (#8) and a calf.

These lines make up the shapes that make the animal look like that specific animal. When sculpting, I build a framework with these lines that make up the shapes. I make them three dimensional and then I will fill in using these lines for the flow of the wire.

Picture 3.2 Several of the examples shown in Picture 3.1 with the photos from which the lines were taken.

Photo by Deb Ritch

1.

4.

5.

6.

Photo by Deb Ritch

8.

13

The shape the lines create will determine the look of an animal. Note the differences of the horse heads in Pictures 3.3 and 3.4. See how different each head can be? Note the difference between the adult horses and the foal.

These differences in shape help you create an individual, a portrait or show the difference in breeds.

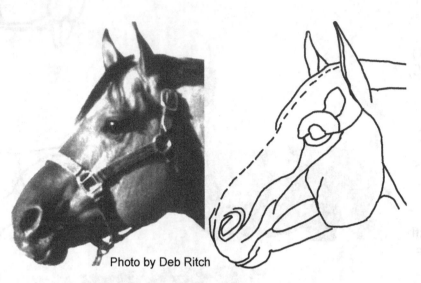

Photo by Deb Ritch

Picture 3.3 Close-up photo of horse head and drawing, showing lines that can be used.

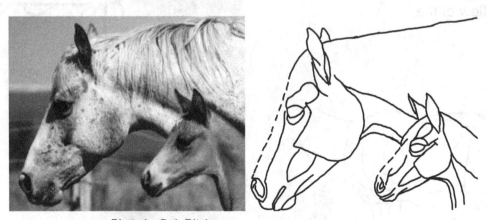

Photo by Deb Ritch

Picture 3.4 Close-up photos of head and neck of a mare and foal and a drawing showing the lines that can be used when starting a sculpture.

The dotted lines in the drawings indicate the outside of the piece and are not necessarily part of the frame and will be part of the fill-in.

I find it is important to follow the muscle, bone, and hair movement with the lines, depending on what my artistic eye sees in the area.

Examples:
- Horse Head (Picture 3.3) primarily follows the bone
- Horse Neck (Picture 3.4) follows the muscle
- Horse Flank follows the hair
- Horse Body follows the muscle and/or ribs, depending on the area portrayed (See Pictures 3.5 and 3.6)

The primary lines can be different (See Pictures 3.5 and 3.6) and still represent the same animal. Sometimes the difference in the shapes or lines will show the uniqueness of an adult or a baby. Often they are used to depict the personality of a specific animal.

Photo by Deb Ritch

Picture 3.5 Lines for the side of an adult horse. This and Picture 3.6 show that the primary lines can be somewhat different and still work for the same animal.

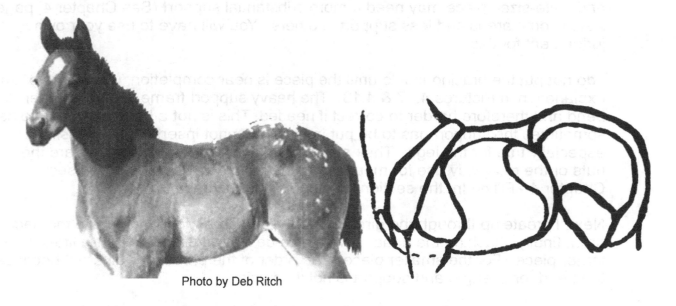

Photo by Deb Ritch

Picture 3.6 Lines for the side of a foal (young horse) This picture and Picture 3.5 show the lines can be somewhat different and still work for the same animal.

I cannot stress enough how essential it is to find the correct lines to follow. These first lines really do determine the final shape and feel of the finished project.

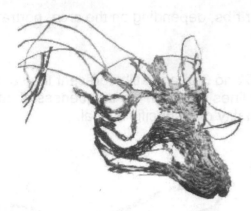

Picture 3.7 Example of the head for a Rocky Mountain Big Horn Sheep.

Once the lines are determined, make a framework in three dimensions. When creating life-size or larger I usually do this in parts, the head first and then the legs. I find that if I first do the head, I can make the remaining parts in proportion. But if I do the body first, somehow the head gets too big. This is just a quirk of mine and may not make a difference to you. For small, tabletop pieces, I do the head, then body, including the neck, and the legs last.

The finished product will be strong even though it may need a supporting frame. The size of the support is determined by the size of the finished piece. A small tabletop piece may not need any support, a larger piece may need 1/4 inch rod and a life-sized piece may need a more substantial support (See Chapter 4, page 23) in some areas and less support in others. You will have to use your own judgement for this.

I do not put the bracing inside until the piece is near completion. (See more of an explanation in Pictures 4.17 & 4.18. The heavy support frame is much harder to bend and therefore harder to correct if needed. This is not a hard and fast rule as sometimes the support has to be put in first if I cannot insert it later. This is especially true for the legs. Their support is put in at the beginning, as are the nuts or the rod I may use for mounting to the base (For the nuts or rod see Chapter 4 - Filling In, the section on mounting to the base on page 23).

Next, I create up through the girth, then the flank areas, continuing into the neck area, finally attaching the head. The above-described process is for a life-size or larger piece. For the smaller pieces, the order of the process is different because the need for strength and support is not as crucial.

Once the framework is established in lines, add temporary supports (See Picture 3.8 and 3.9) to make sure the lines stay in place. These are temporary and will be taken out as the area is filled in. I also place guidelines to make sure I fill in the form with the correct contour.

For example, I will put in temporary guidelines (barbed wire or other wire can be used for the guidelines) to suggest the roundness of the belly or any other area where the shape will be inward or outward between the primary lines. (See the Pictures 3.8 and 3.9 below.) The dotted lines are indicated by the arrows and are the supports and used as guidelines to help keep the contours' shapes when filling in between the lines.

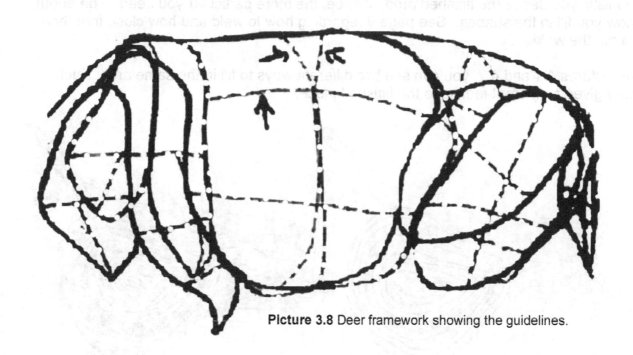

Picture 3.8 Deer framework showing the guidelines.

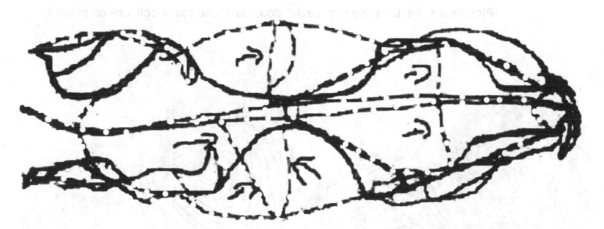

Picture 3.9 Another view of guidelines.

These guidelines really help. **Remember to take the guidelines out before completion, or they will show through the finished piece and ruin the flow of your lines.**

Chapter 4
Filling in the Project ▼ Support Frame ▼ Mounting to a Base ▼ Making an Eye

Filling in the Project

After determining the lines that create the shapes, begin filling in the shapes. The more realistic you desire the finished product to be, the more particular you need to be about how you fill in the shapes. See page 9 regarding how to weld and how close together to put the welds.

In Pictures 4.1 and 4.2, you can see two different ways to fill in the same area. Each way gives a different feeling to the finished piece.

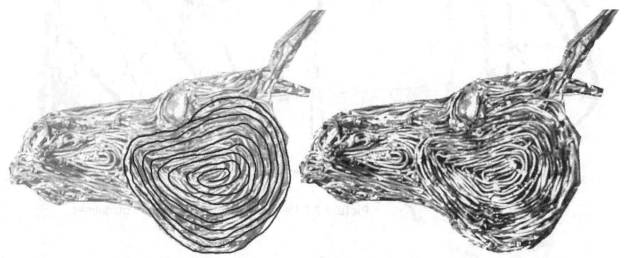

Picture 4.1 Fill by going in a "circle" does not make the cheek look as natural.

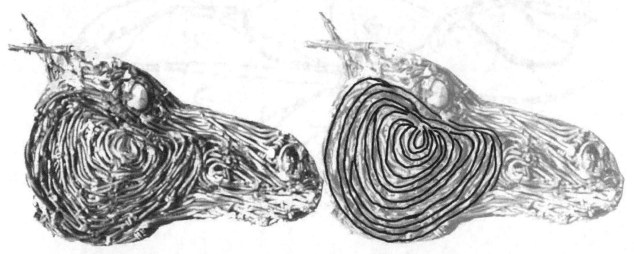

Picture 4.2 To achieve a more natural look, fill by going with the line and shape of the cheekbone.

In pictures 4.9 through 4.15 you can see more examples of different ways to fill in. Note the different feel each flow gives to the sculpture.

The following pictures, 4.3 through 4.8, will show how I filled in the head in Picture 4.2. In Chapter 5, see more information on blending and filling in to make the sculpture have more of a realistic feel. The fill is one *strand* of wire in thickness (a strand made up of 2 wires twisted together). The sculpture is hollow inside. If you weld close enough together (every 2 inches or so) this surface will become very strong.

Picture 4.3 #1 is the start area where two wires of a twist of barbed wire are welded in as if one wire. Number 2 shows an example where the wire left a gap; when that happens I will weld a separate wire in to fill the gap.

Picture 4.3 shows an area where the wire does not fill in smoothly and tightly to the adjacent wires. A barb often causes a gap as the barbs sometimes get in the way. When that happens I cut them out with the torch as I go along. What makes the wonderful texture is the twist of the wire, not necessarily the barbs. Picture 4.4 shows how I welded a short piece of wire to fill in the gap.

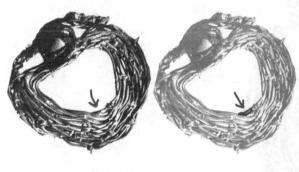

Picture 4.4 shows the short wire that was welded into the gap.

Picture 4.5 Some of the lines of the fill .

On this piece, I started the fill by going around only part of the shape (See Picture 4.5). I began the wire to the side of and below the eye, circled around the cheek area, and ended with the two twisted wires bent and welded as one wire on the other side and below the eye. (See more instructions in Chapter 5 - Blending.)

99

Do not stop or start in the same place when blending. Sometimes an area, such as the flank of the horse, should have a stopping line. But normally I do not want all wires to start or stop at the same place.

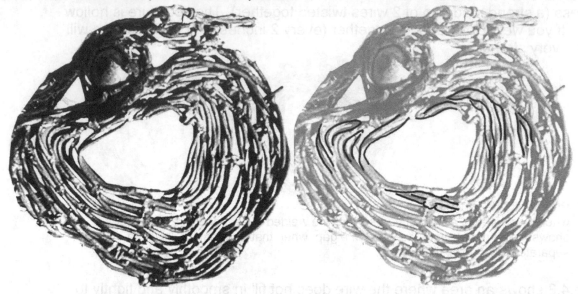

Picture 4.6 #4 Do not always stop in the same area or on the same line. Here I went around the cheek and beneath the eye instead of starting and stopping on the opposite side.

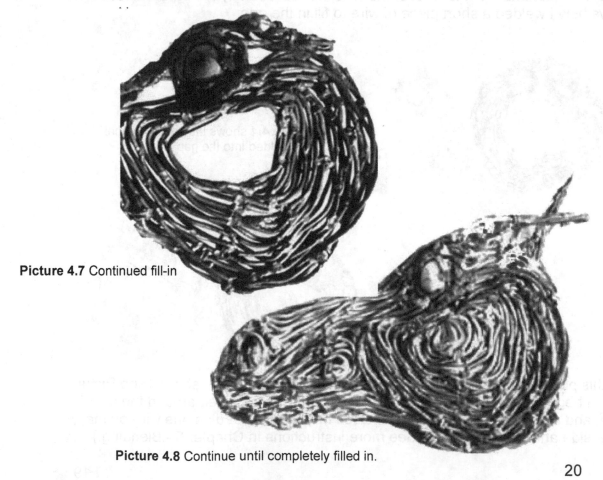

Picture 4.7 Continued fill-in

Picture 4.8 Continue until completely filled in.

Pictures 4.9 through 4.11 are three different examples of ways to fill in a horse head. Each way achieves a different feeling of movement because of the direction the wire runs. There are always several different choices for filling in the shapes of your project. Pick the one that you like the best.

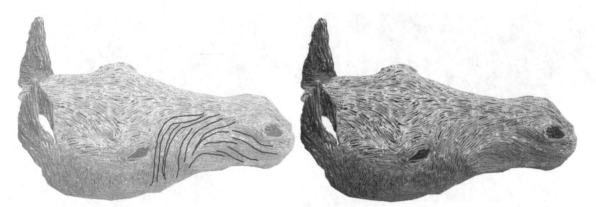

Picture 4.9 The lines come from the bottom of the cheek up and over to the top of the nose.

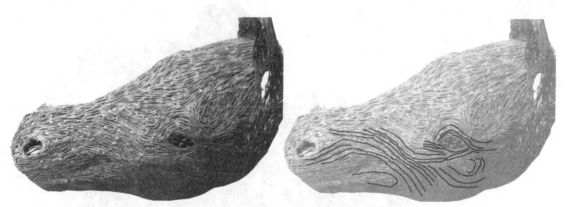

Picture 4.10 The lines coming from under the eye and then up over the bridge of the nose towards the nose.

Picture 4.11 The lines come from the cheek up to meet the lines coming forward from under the eye and blend together into the nasal area.

21

In Pictures 4.12 and 4.13 you can see an example of filling in and not blending. This is one of my early pieces and I had not figured out how to blend the change of directions. Because it is consistent throughout the complete piece, I think it works. Now I prefer to blend.

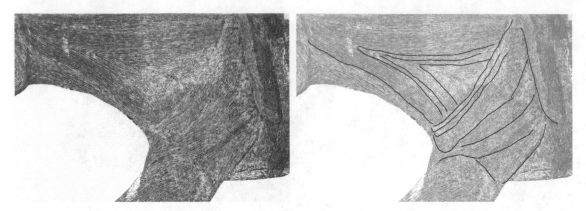

Picture 4.12 This picture shows the lines in one of my first sculptures. You can see that there are many places where that rows of lines come to a complete stop in the same area. They would be much more realistic if the ends were staggered so they were blended. (See more about blending in Chapter 5.)

Picture 4.13 A larger view of this sculpture entitled *"Into the Homestretch."*

22

Pictures 4.14 and 4.15 show a sculpture that is a good example of blending. In this sculpture, there are few abrupt stopping places in the movement of the wire. Consequently, it has better flow in the movement of the lines, portraying power and motion.

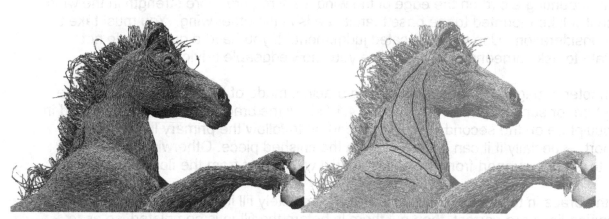

Picture 4.14 In one of my later sculptures I blended the lines throughout the sculpture.

Picture 4.15 *"Cavallo Mustang,"* barbed wire horse sculpture standing 16 hands high

23

Support Frame

The size of the support is determined by the size of the sculpture and the position in which the subject is portrayed. An animal standing firmly on all four legs will not require as much support as a four-legged animal posed on one or two legs.

If I am mounting a bird on the edge of the wing it will require more strength in the wing which it will be mounted to the base than it needs in the other wing. You must take this into consideration. Use your educated judgement. If you have a question do not hesitate to ask someone who could give you knowledgeable advice.

In Chapter 3, page 16, I talk about putting bracing, made of heavier metal, inside the sculpture for support. Pictures 4.16 and 4.17 show the bracing I put in before I filled in the sculpture on the second side. It is important to follow the primary lines for this support, especially if it can be see through the finished piece. Otherwise you will be able to see the support from the outside and it will detract from the flow of the lines.

Put the brace in the second side before you completely fill it in. Make sure the beginning lines are correct, then put them in before the fill-in is completed, so as to have access to the area.

I firmly weld the brace to the sculpture in several places along the support rod making sure the weld includes different parts of the sculpture. Welding to more than one wire increases its strength.

If you are sure you have the initial lines and the shape correct then weld the strengthening supports in at the beginning.

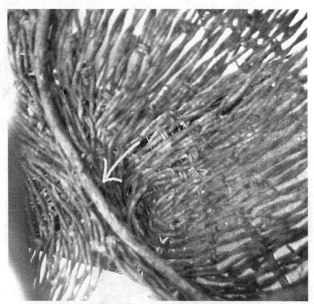

Picture 4.17 The rod (see arrow) is the brace that has been welded inside for strength.

Picture 4.16 This is another example of a strengthening rod.

Mounting to the Base

There are millions of ways to attach the sculpture to a base. In addition, there are many choices for bases. Some of my larger pieces do not have a base. The owners wanted them to appear as if they were in the wild.

Therefore, the choice of how you connect your sculpture to the mount will be determined by the kind of base you wish to create.

Pictures 4.18 and 4.19 illustrate how I often weld a nut inside the bottom of the foot (the example is a horse hoof) of the animal. Weld the nut firmly to the strengthening rod. This rod will go up through the leg and be firmly welded to the hoof itself. Be sure that the nut will lie flat on the ground with the bolt perpendicular to the base.

In picture 4.18 and 4.19, #1 is the hoof, #2 is the strengthening rod, and #3 is the nut. The size of the nut and rod are determined by the size of your sculpture.

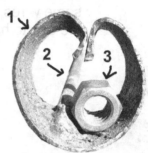

Picture 4.18 This shows the nut, #3, and reinforcement bar, #2, placed early in the construction of the foot. The nut is used to mount the finished sculpture to the base.

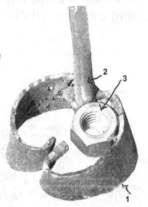

Picture 4.19 View seen from the bottom.

Making an Eye

I use a plate that is ½ inch, or thicker with a hole (#1) cut into it. I take a steel ball bearing (#2) the size of the eye I want to make and place it on top of a piece of sheet steel and over the hole (#1). The eye is shaped by the use of a press. I have a 20-ton press that I purchased from *Harbor Freight Tools*. This will press out a bubble (the eye shape) into the sheet steel. If you do not have a press, you can heat the metal sheet and beat out an indentation in the shape of the eye (#3.) I cut this bubble out (#4) and that is my eye. I then weld it into the sculpture.

Picture 4.20 (#1) Thick metal with a hole into which I press a steel ball (#2) or alternately, you can beat the metal with a hammer to create the eye shape (#3) in sheet steel. #4 shows the hole from which the eye was cut.

Chapter 5 - Blending Techniques

To make the movement in a sculpture smooth and have the lines flow more into another direction without a stopping point, one must blend the wire. Here are three techniques that accomplish this:

1)   Make the two wire ends of a strand* connect into one wire by twisting them so only one wire shows. Then weld it onto a single wire, making sure the bottom wire is directly under the top wire. This will continue the flow of the line.

2)   Separate the two wire ends of a strand.* Weld one wire end to one wire and the other end to a wire in a different area.

3)   One wire connects different areas together. Make sure that the flow of the wire is as you desire it. Also, do not weld consistently into the same wires unless you want to create a stopping point that causes the eye to halt rather than flowing over the whole piece.

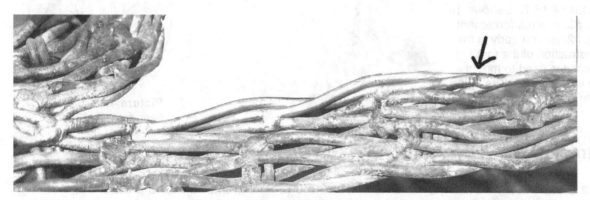

Picture 5.1 Arrow points to technique #1. Two wires from one strand* of barbed wire are welded into one wire.

Technique #1 is shown in Pictures 5.1 and 5.2. The two wires from a strand* of barbed wire (wires #1 and #2) flow into the one wire (wire #3) that is part of another strand*. The arrow points to welding area. Picture 5.2 is a close-up illustration of the area where the two wires are welded into one wire.

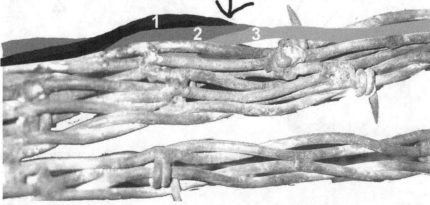

Picture 5.2 Closeup of 5.1 illustrates where the two wires (#1 & #2) are welded together to attach to a third wire (#3).

*A strand of barbed wire is comprised of two wires that are twisted together.

Pictures 5.3 and 5.4 are examples of technique #2. Each of the two wires of a strand of barbed wire are welded to different areas. This will keep the lines flowing.

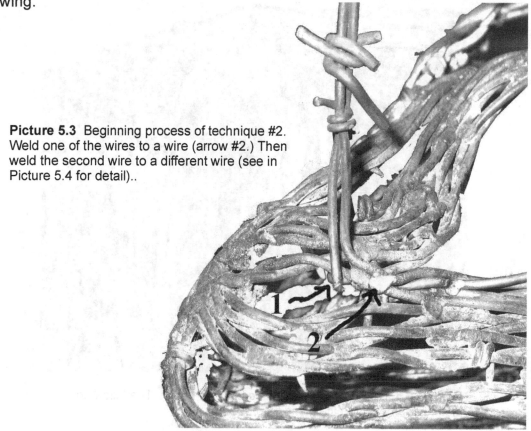

Picture 5.3 Beginning process of technique #2. Weld one of the wires to a wire (arrow #2.) Then weld the second wire to a different wire (see in Picture 5.4 for detail)..

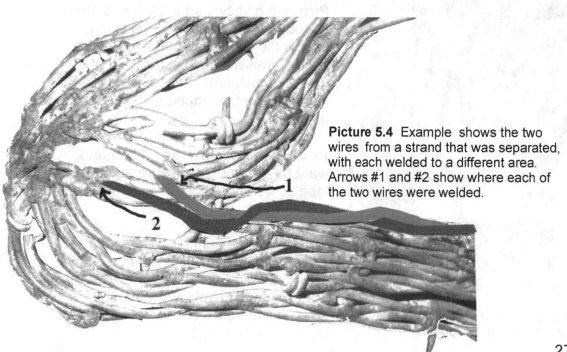

Picture 5.4 Example shows the two wires from a strand that was separated, with each welded to a different area. Arrows #1 and #2 show where each of the two wires were welded.

Below is an example of technique #3, which is using one wire to continue the flow so you don't create a stopping place.

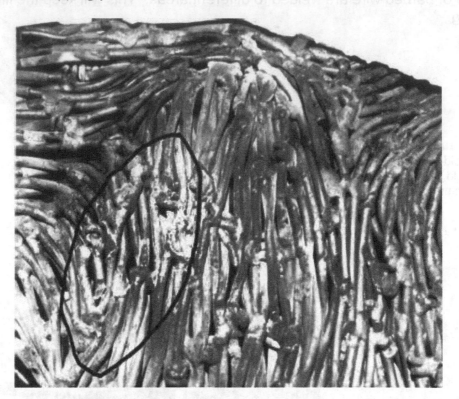

Picture 5.5 Circled area needs to be blended better. The following pictures demonstrate the blending process.

Picture 5.6 Close-up of area that will be fixed in Pictures 5.7 and 5.8.

Picture 5.5 shows an area that is still a bit rough and interrupting the visual flow of the line. The bottom left of the circled area will be fixed in the following pictures. There is a very large welded area that impedes the flow of the line.

Picture 5.6 is a close-up of the part I want to correct. The illustrated parts labeled #1 and #2 are the areas I want to connect to one another.

Wire #1 will be connected to wire #2 by a single wire which will continue the line. This will cover the large welded spot inside the circle to create a smooth line flow.

28

Picture 5.7 shows that one wire did not flow. The top end of the wire (#1) welds to the wire above it and the bottom end #3 welds to the wire below it (#2). This will make the area flow and look smooth.

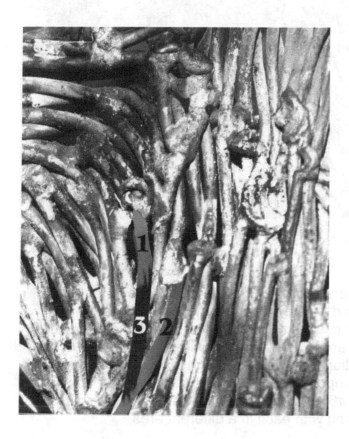

Picture 5.7 This is an illustration of the corrected area. # 1 and # 3 are ends of the same wire. This piece of wire is welded over the rough large weld and is attached to wire #2.

Picture 5.8 Close-up of the finished blended area using technique #3.

In some areas I need to use all three of the techniques. Picture 5.9 shows an area of extreme curves. This could stop the visual flow of the lines. Thus, one needs to use all of the techniques, sometimes uses more than one technique on the same strand of wire.

Picture 5.9 An area of extreme curves.

In picture 5.10 I have illustrated and numbered some of the blended areas to make it easier to see what was done. Wires #1 and #2 are two components of the same strand. (A barbed wire strand consists of two wires twisted together.) It would stop the flow if both wires were to stop in the same area. Therefore the wires are separated and wire #1 is welded into a different direction than wire #2, which also continues the flow around the curve. Wire #3 and #4, components of a second strand of barbed wire, are ending in the same area. Wire #5 and #6, comprising the third strand, also split and terminate in separate places, also ending with each in a different area.

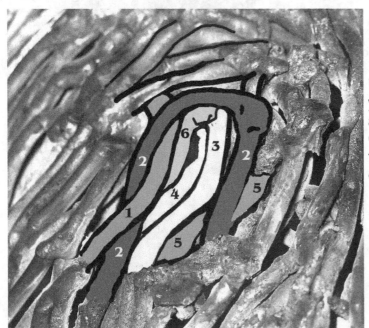

Using these blending techniques as you are welding one wire or a strand at a time is not as difficult as it looks. Choosing the methods and blending the wires comes naturally after a bit of practice.

Picture 5.10 Shows how these wires are blended.

Pictures 5.10 through 5.12 are more examples of different areas that have been blended using the three techniques. Note that the original picture is on the left and the illustration of the blend on the right in these examples.

(Photo)
Picture 5.11   Example of blending technique #1
(Illustration)

 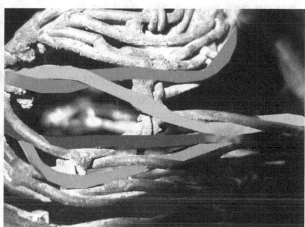

(Photo)
Picture 5.12   Examples of blending technique #2
(Illustration)

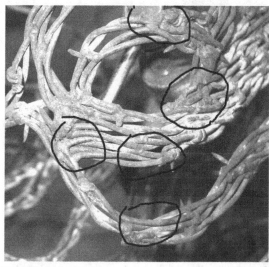 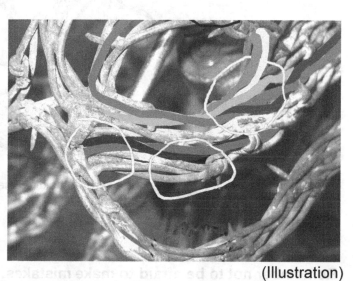

(Photo)
(Illustration)
Picture 5.13 Several examples of different ways to blend. Can you pick them out?

Chapter 6 - Creation of the Horse Body

The initial lines are always very important. They should show action and movement, and be in correct proportion.

RESEARCH! Look at live animals that you are going to represent in your creation to get the proportions or look for books that shows you this. When looking at another artist's work make sure the proportions are correct.

The correct proportions are essential when creating realistically.

Held by my vise

6.1 Picture of the left side showing the beginning wires. It is being held by my favorite vise.

6.2 Here I'm holding the right side showing the beginning wires.

Remember not to be afraid to make mistakes. As you will see I made several mistakes which I later corrected.

From here I begin to fill in. Sometimes the fill-in works without any corrections. On small pieces, it is often hard to get the wire to flow correctly the first time.

Picture 6.3 shows how the wires lay the first time around. This piece is small and therefore has many tight twists and turns. All the wires have to lay very flat and smooth or it will not look right. On a large piece it often lays in correctly initially with no need for corrections.

In Picture 6.3, #1 marks where the under part of the neck meets the movement of the shoulder. The wire had to come to a stop. Area #2 has wires that do not blend and will have to be blended. Area #3 also has wires that need to be blended. There are also areas with holes that need to be filled in to make this piece nice and smooth.

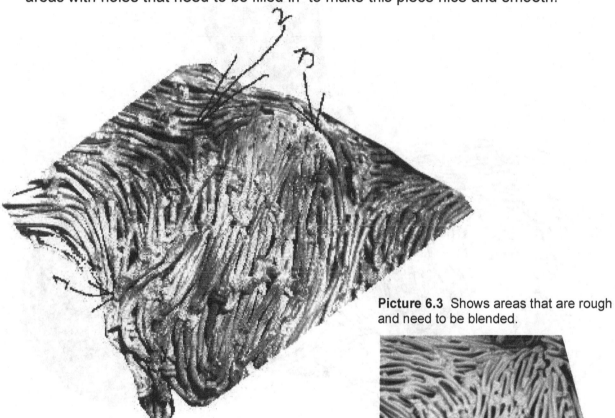

Picture 6.3 Shows areas that are rough and need to be blended.

I could have chosen to leave these areas. However, if left as it lay originally, the finished product would not have been as realistic. I prefer realism, so I work to fill in and blend.

I blended these areas and smoothed them. To see how this was done and for more ideas concerning how to blend, see Chapter 5.

Picture 6.4 Same area as shown in Picture 6.3 after it has been blended. Note my "BJH" signature as well.

I work with the piece attached firmly to a vise. A great deal of pushing and pulling is needed to get the wire into the proper shape, so it has to be held firmly by something strong.

The vise I am using for this piece is my favorite (see Picture 1.14, Chapter 1-Tools). It will move from horizontal to vertical position. It helps to be able to have the piece in the different positions as it makes it easier to weld the sculpture in all areas.

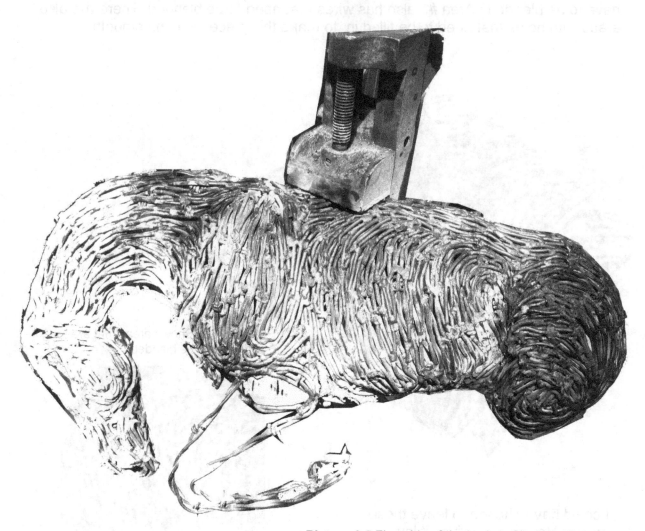

Picture 6.5 First side of the body is filled in. The sculpture is held in place by my favorite vise.

Here I have completed the left side of the body first (See Picture 6.5), including the head, neck and body (but not the legs). I then proceed to the other side of the body.

In Picture 6.6 the initial lines for the right side of the neck are indicated to by arrows. #1 is the line that denotes the throat area of the neck. #2 shows how the second wire is then welded along the original line, and so on until the complete neck is filled in.

In picture 6.6, the piece is attached to the vise by the ear.

If there are areas where it's inaccessible to weld when held in the vise, I weld an extra piece to the sculpture in an area that will enable me to put the sculpture in a position that will let me to reach the more difficult areas. I remove this extra piece when it is no longer needed.

After all of the body is completely filled in I start the legs.

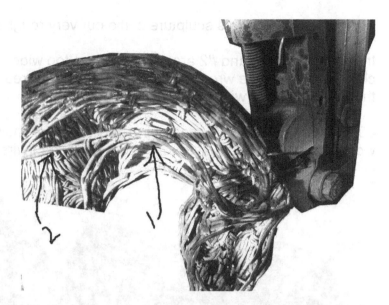

Picture 6.6 Right side of the neck beginning lines.

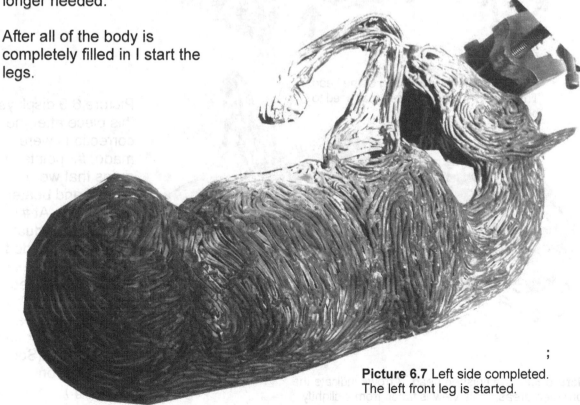

Picture 6.7 Left side completed. The left front leg is started.

Picture 6.8 is another example of an area that was not correct the first time. Especially when making a small piece, an area often has to be re-worked two or three different times in to order make it correct.

The initial head for this sculpture came out very rough and incorrect in several areas.

In Picture 6.8, #1 and #2 are areas that are too wide. Also, #2 points to the horse's chin, which is in the wrong place. I heated these areas red-hot and then beat them into the desired shape with a hammer.

#3 is an area that needs more wire. It is too small; however one strand of barbed wire would make it too big. Instead, I use one piece of wire to fill in that area.

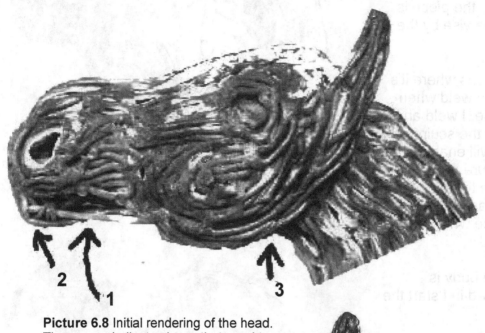

Picture 6.8 Initial rendering of the head. The arrows indicate places that need to be corrected.

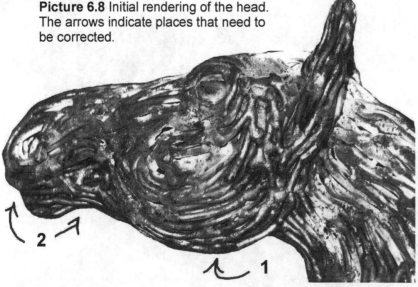

Picture 6.9 The finished head. Arrows indicate the corrected areas. This view is taken from a slightly different angle than Picture 6.8.

Picture 6.9 displays this piece after the corrections were made. #2 points to areas that were heated and beaten into shape. At #1, several individual wires were welded into place to make it wider and shaped correctly. I also blended the area where the neck and head attach. (See Chapter 5, on blending.)

Picture 6.11 shows the beginning of the
left rear leg before the corrections. The
arrows show where there are holes that
will be filled in, either with a strand of
barbed wire or with a single wire.

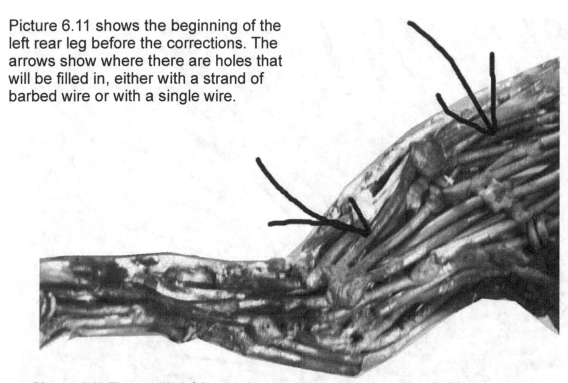

Picture 6.11 The outside left leg needs
to be re-worked. The arrows point to holes
that need to be filled.

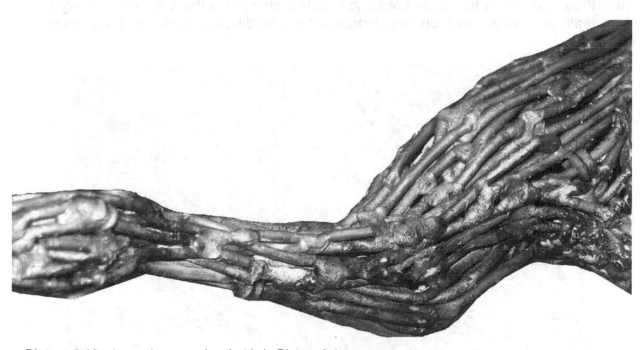

Picture 6.12 shows the same leg that is in Picture 6.1
after all the fill-in and blending has been completed.

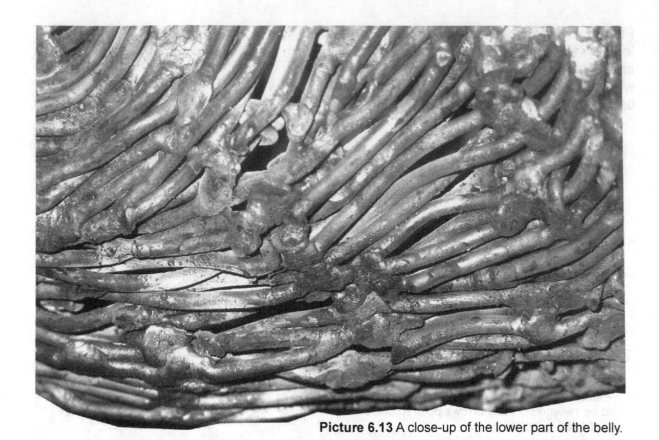

Picture 6.13 A close-up of the lower part of the belly.

Pictures 6.13 and 6.14 are close-up pictures of the belly area that show the many twists and turns, giving the feeling of shape and muscle movement. Both of these pictures show the piece after it has been filled and blended, smoothing the area and making it more realistic. Can you pick out the blended areas and different techniques that were used?

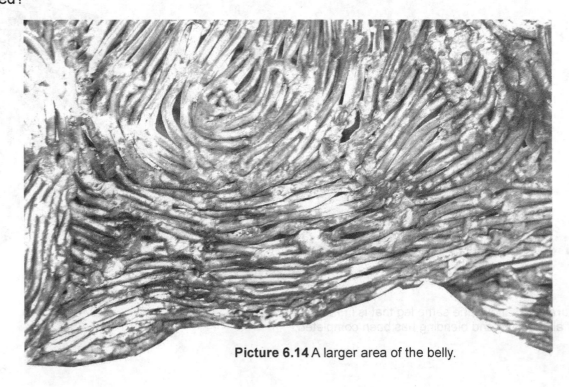

Picture 6.14 A larger area of the belly.

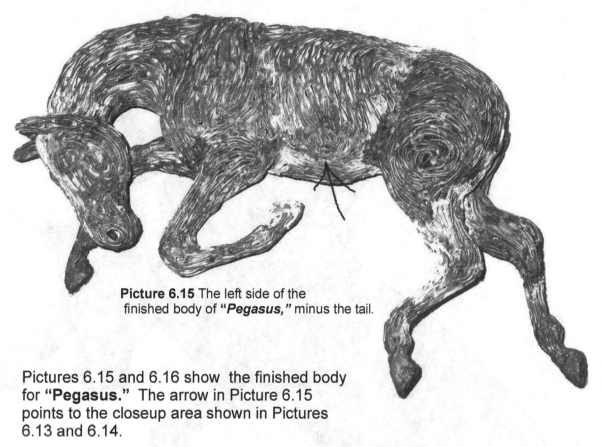

Picture 6.15 The left side of the
finished body of **"*Pegasus,*"** minus the tail.

Pictures 6.15 and 6.16 show the finished body
for **"Pegasus."** The arrow in Picture 6.15
points to the closeup area shown in Pictures
6.13 and 6.14.

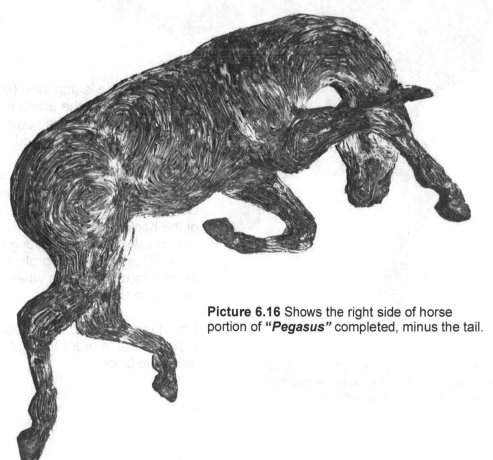

Picture 6.16 Shows the right side of horse
portion of **"*Pegasus*"** completed, minus the tail.

Next, the mane is attached (see Picture 6.17) and the brace for the tail is put in. The tail will be completed after the wings are attached.

I should have put the tail brace in before the fill-in was completed. Consequently, I had to cut out a part of the back in order to weld a 1/4-inch rod for the tail brace in along the back. This rod, which protrudes a few inches from the rear, is where I will attach the tail.

I must remember to fill the back area that I cut out in order to weld the rod along the back.

Picture 6.17 This is the completed body of the horse section of *"Pegasus"* minus the tail. The brace of the tail is shown here.

Part V
Wings

Chapter 7 - Creating Wings

Now to make wings for **"Pegasus."** I will use an eagle's wings as a model, therefore I found a good picture of a real eagle with its wings out-stretched. I used my computer to enlarge the photo to the size I needed for the wings, printed it and cut it out. This way I am sure that I have the correct placement of the feathers. I could do this without the use of the computer by drawing it out, but this is faster. Since I possess the skill to do it myself, I consider this assistance from technology acceptable. (See Picture 7.1.)

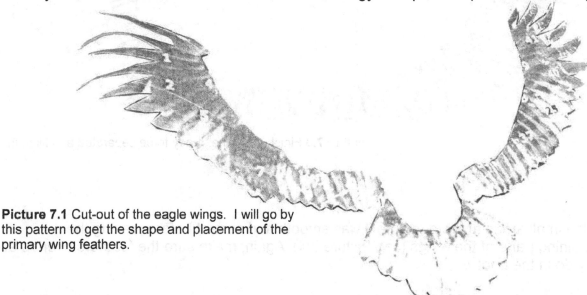

Picture 7.1 Cut-out of the eagle wings. I will go by this pattern to get the shape and placement of the primary wing feathers.

I first make an outline of the outer feathers with barbed wire. Birds feathers overlap in a specific way and it is important that my sculptured wing feathers overlap the same way. That requires that the overlapping the feathers lay so that the edge of the feather that shows on the bottom side is toward the body and edge that shows on the top side is away from the body.

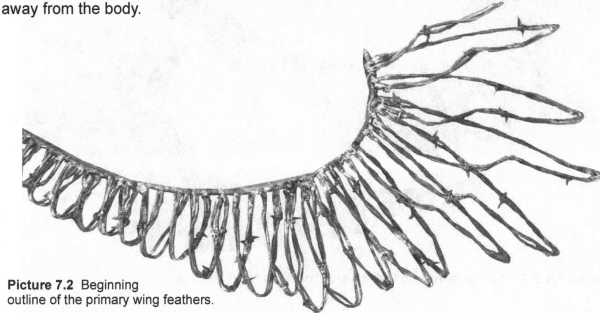

Picture 7.2 Beginning outline of the primary wing feathers.

When making the outline of the wings, I left the two sides of the wingspan attached (see Picture 7.3) to be sure the overall shape and angle would be correct. I then cut them apart as it was too cumbersome to fill in when it was all one piece. I found filling in one side at a time is a lot easier.

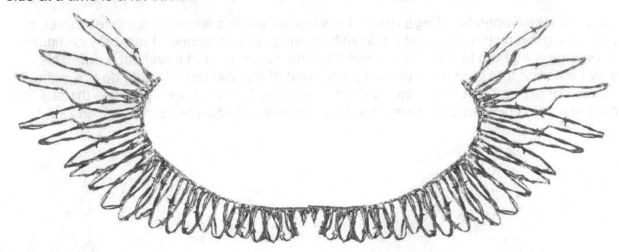

Picture 7.3 Finished outline, ready to be separated and filled in.

I filled in all areas and made sure it was smooth and correct before making the remaining parts of the wings (see Picture 7.4). Again, make sure the feathers overlap as they do in the photo.

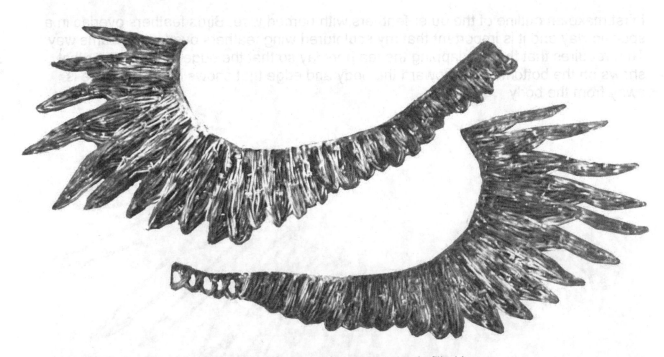

Picture 7.4 Both of the primary wing feathers are almost completely filled in.

42

Fill-in for Feathers

There are several ways to fill in feathers. I chose to fill them in leaving the outline and not putting in a rachis (central shaft) as in Pictures 7.5 and 7.6.

Another way to fill in a feather is to use a wire for the rachis, and then attach the wire the way the barbs of the feather lie, as in Picture 7.7. After all the barbs of the feathers are made then the outline is discarded. This creates very realistic feathers. However, It takes a long time to make a wing this way.

Picture 7.5 The fill in for the large feathers in *"Pegasus."*

Picture 7.7 Another suggested way to fill in feathers so they are structurally more like a real feather.

Picture 7.6 The small feathers fill in *"Pegasus."*

Next I made the lines (see arrow in Picture 7.9) for attaching each row of feathers. I will fill in the under side of the wing first. I chose to make the under side first, because the wing will be bent and curved into the shape of an eagle's and it is easier to make this happen if the under side is filled in first. It will bend easier this way.

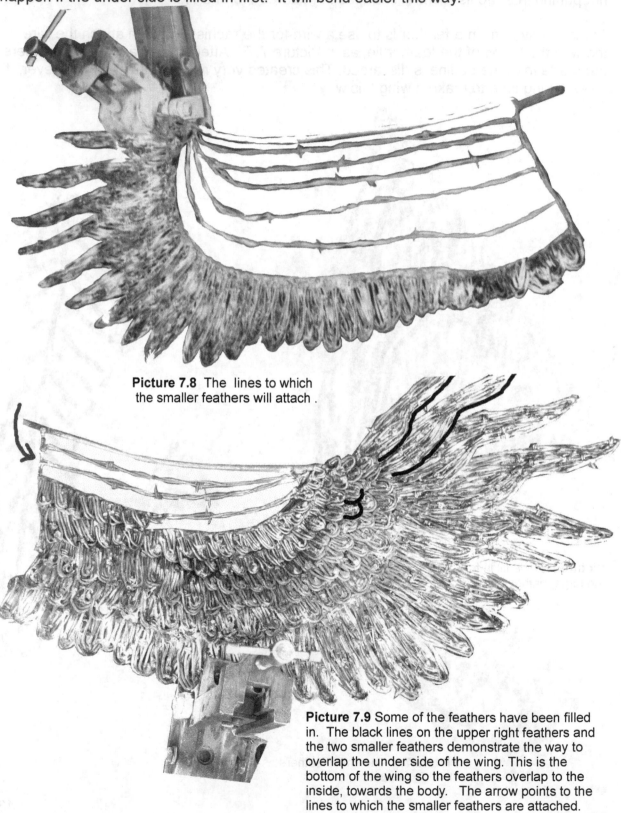

Picture 7.8 The lines to which the smaller feathers will attach .

Picture 7.9 Some of the feathers have been filled in. The black lines on the upper right feathers and the two smaller feathers demonstrate the way to overlap the under side of the wing. This is the bottom of the wing so the feathers overlap to the inside, towards the body. The arrow points to the lines to which the smaller feathers are attached.

44

I want to mount this piece by a wing to give the impression that *"Pegasus"* is flying. At this point the mounting pipes need to be inserted. There will be stainless steel rods, part of the base, which will slip into these pipes when the sculpture is completed.

I chose stainless steel rods to mount *"Pegasus"* because their greater strength for their size will hold the sculpture in the air.

After the pipes are installed where I want them, I closed the top ends of these pipes by pinching them together and welding that area. This will not allow the rods to go through any further. Next I filled in the top of the wings with feathers, covering the pipe mounts, which will secure the pipes between the top and bottom of the wing feathers..

Picture 7.10 The bottom side of the wing is completed. In this picture the wing is turned over to fill in the top of the wing. This also shows the pipe that is being inserted to attach the base to *"Pegasus"*. These pipes will lie in between the top and bottom of the wing when the sculpture is completed.

The feathers on the top side overlap the opposite direction. That means the outside edge of each feather overlaps away from the body, so they show on top to the outside. This is an important feature that needs to be correct.

After all the feathers are filled in on both sides, I will weld feathers onto the upper side along the edge, bend them over the front of the wing and attach them to the under side. This will complete the wing (see arrow in Picture 7.11).

Picture 7.11 The wing has been filled in on both the upper and under sides. The arrow points to the feathers that will be bent over the front part of the wing and welded to the underside. This will finish the wing.

Chapter 8 - The Finishing Touches

The wings and the horse body are now completed but separate. Next the wings are attached to the horse and feathers are filled in as needed to transition from wing feathers to the horse's shoulders (see Picture 8.1 and 8.2). (If I were creating a bird, the wings would be attached to the bird's body and feathers created to transition from wing to body.)

Picture 8.1 Shows the top view of the wings attached to the horse and filled in to create a transition to the body.

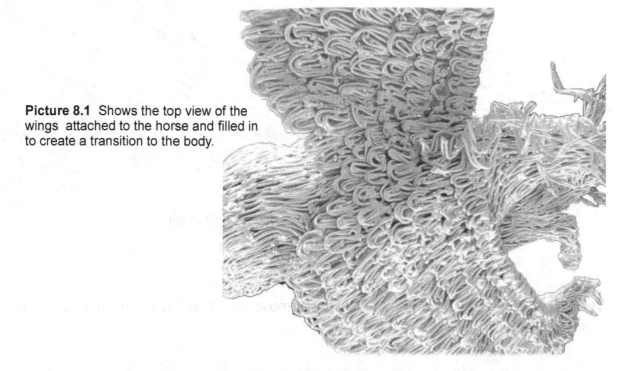

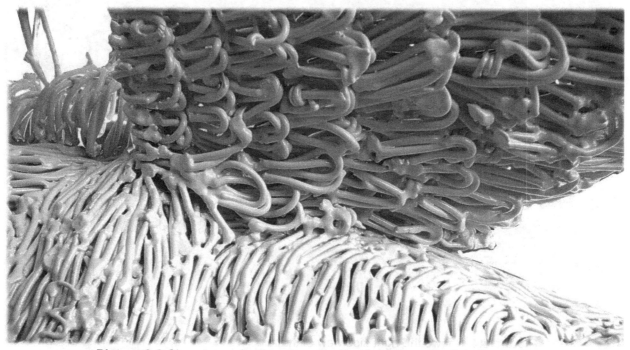

Picture 8.2 Close-up under the wings shows where they attach to the body.

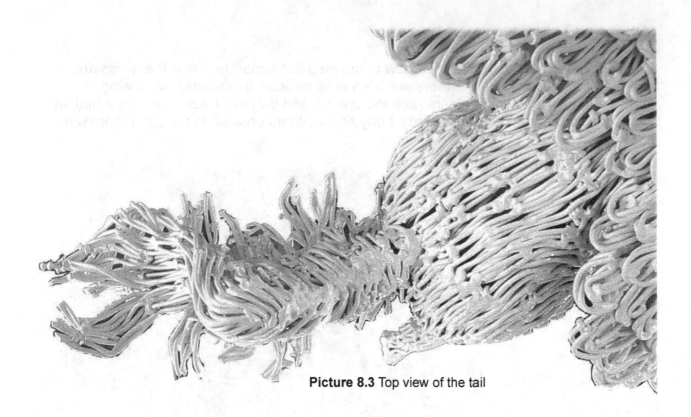

Picture 8.3 Top view of the tail

The last item I created was the tail. I wanted movement that depicts his playful action. See this tail in Pictures 8.3 and 8.4.

Picture 8.4 Shows the right side view of the tail.

To mount *"Pegasus"* to a base, there are two small open-end pieces of pipe welded in between the outer part of the right wing with the opening on the top. Two pieces of stainless steel rod will slide into these pipes. (See the rods in Picture 8.5 on the bottom right and Picture 7.10 to see the installation of the pipes the rods slide into.) These rods then connect the sculpture to the base and are part of the design (See Picture 8.6).

Picture 8.5 Top of *"Pegasus"* showing the rods that slide into the pipes that were placed in the end of the right wing.

Now, to make the base for mounting: I want it to give the feeling of the flight of **"Pegasus"** and not be something heavy, or a design that would take your eye away from **"Pegasus"**. I want to give a hint of clouds, and after making that cloud base and the attachment rods for the sculpture, I felt I needed a transition between the base and the sculpture. After some thought, I decided the stars would work well, especially since **"Pegasus"** is also a constellation.

There are many different ways to mount this piece. I chose this base, made from stainless steel, mounted on wood as it is heavy enough to hold the sculpture safely and not tip over when this sculpture is touched. This is important as **"Pegasus"** will move some when touched. The stainless steel is strong enough to hold **"Pegasus"** aloft!

Picture 8.6 The finished sculpture is named **"Steed of the Gods"**. The completed sculpture is 57½"H x 35"W x 30"D. The wingspan is 47" and the horse is 14" at the withers.

Part VI
Long Hair, Wool, and Fur
Step-by-step Creation of a Life-size Fox
Finished sculpture is unnamed
Size 42"L x 17"H x 11"W

Chapter 9 - The creation of a life-size fox.

Creating the look of long hair, wool or fur is a very different process than creating short-haired or hairless animals. The lines are not as crucial. However, I go with the flow of the hair. The shape is the most important item to remember when creating long hair. I start by making the shape of the outer form. The shape needs to be of the size it would be were the animal skinned. If I make the initial form as large as the animal is with all of its hair, the finished piece will be much too large and can lose much of the actual shape.

Pictures 9.1 and 9.2 show the beginning outline of a fox minus the legs. The rear of the sculpture has the beginning lines to which the hair will be attached. This is similar to the way to make the feathers of a bird (see Chapter 7). The arrows point to these beginning lines.

I make lines all around the sculptures about 1 to 1 ½ inches apart, depending on the size of the finished piece. In a smaller sculpture, the lines need to be very close.

The lines are determined somewhat by following the lines of the fox in the way I determine the lines for a short-haired animal as explained in Chapter 3.

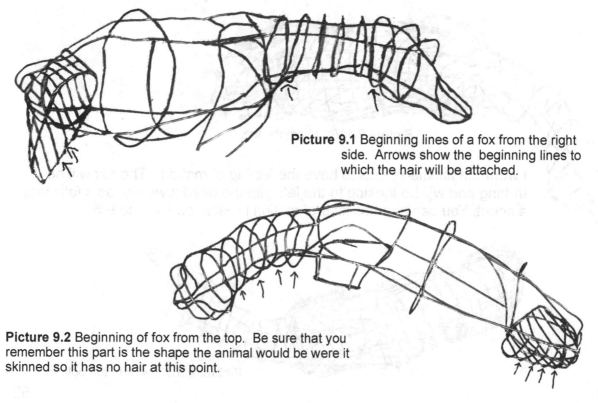

Picture 9.1 Beginning lines of a fox from the right side. Arrows show the beginning lines to which the hair will be attached.

Picture 9.2 Beginning of fox from the top. Be sure that you remember this part is the shape the animal would be were it skinned so it has no hair at this point.

All the areas where the fox has long hair will now be covered with the lines to which I will attach the hair. (See Pictures 9.2 through 9.4.) As with most long-haired animals, the fox has some areas that are not long-haired, such as the nose and parts of the legs. These areas of short hair are filled in the same way as the short-haired or hairless animals and do not need the lines that are used for attaching the long hair.

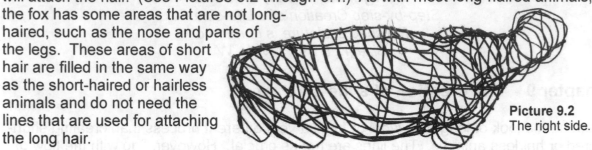

Picture 9.2
The right side.

In Picture 9.3 the arrows point to the indentations where the back and shoulder meet and where the belly and chest meet. **At this stage the shape needs to be over-emphasized and the features exaggerated.** By that I mean the shape is indented more than the finished shape will be. This is because the addition of the hair will lessen the curves and smooth the shape to a large degree.

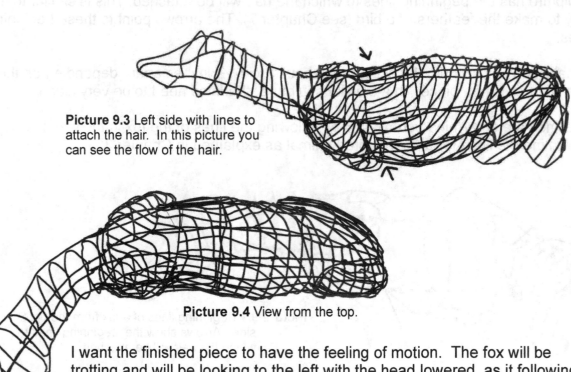

Picture 9.3 Left side with lines to attach the hair. In this picture you can see the flow of the hair.

Picture 9.4 View from the top.

I want the finished piece to have the feeling of motion. The fox will be trotting and will be looking to the left with the head lowered as it following a scent. You can see this kind of motion in Pictures 9.4 and 9.5.

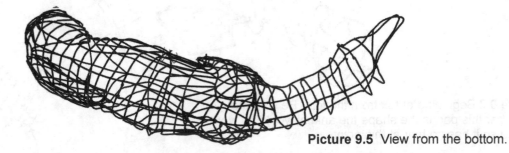

Picture 9.5 View from the bottom.

52

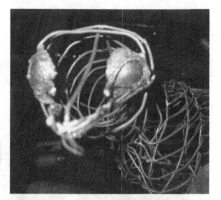

Picture 9.6 Head outline and eyes shown from the front.

Picture 9.6 Side view of the wire outline for the fox head including the eye. (See how to create the eye in Chapter 4, page 25.)

The head has short hair so I make it like the short-haired animal. Since the short hair is not overlapping like most of the rest of the fox, I chose to do it first.

The eyes lie under the skin and hair so they have to be placed in first. (For detail on how to make the eyes see Chapter 4, page 25.) Put the eyes in place and attach firmly all the way around the eye by welding to the wires of the frame. (See Pictures 9.6, 9.7, and 9.8.)

Make sure they are in the correct position. Look carefully at the sources you are using to make this placement. Although it can be changed at any time in the future it will be a lot of work to do so later; therefore, it is best to have it correct in the beginning.

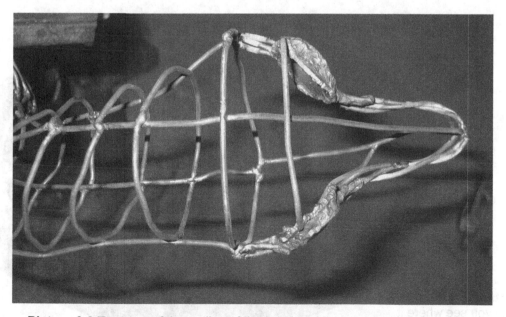

Picture 9.8 Top view of the outline of the head and the mounted eyes.

Pictures 9.9 and 9.10 show
different views of the same
area that needs work.

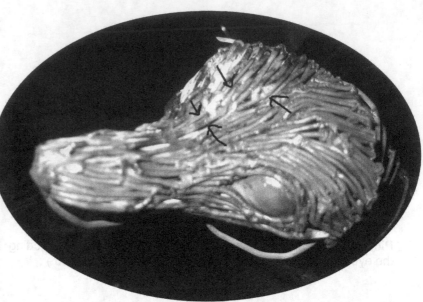

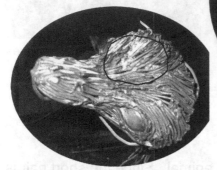

Picture 9.9 Top of head filled in.
The circled area needs more blending.

Picture 9.10 Different view of the top of head filled in.
The arrows point to an area that needs more blending

The first fill-in of the head is complete. The first lines often do not lie smoothly initially.
The circle in Picture 9.9 and the arrows in 9.10 point to an area that did not fill in
completely. I will fill in the rough areas. On a larger piece this may not need to be
blended more. For smaller pieces it often does. The smaller the piece, the harder it is
to get fine detail. In a larger piece, this fine detail is not usually so critical.

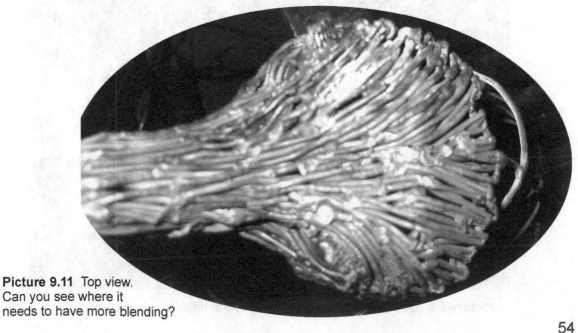

Picture 9.11 Top view.
Can you see where it
needs to have more blending?

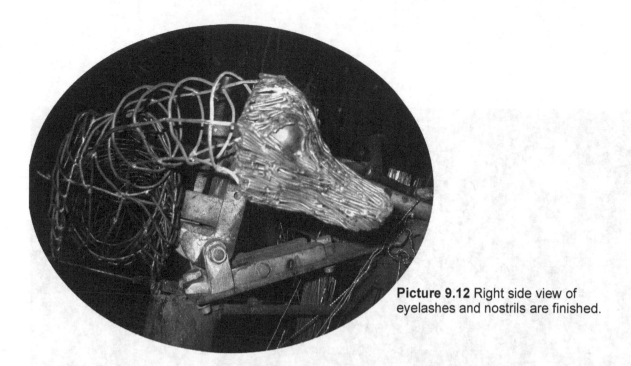

Picture 9.12 Right side view of eyelashes and nostrils are finished.

Once the head fill-in is completed, I added the eyelashes and put more detail in the nostrils, thereby completing the part of the head that is short-haired. Pictures 9.12 and 9.13 show a close-up of these areas.

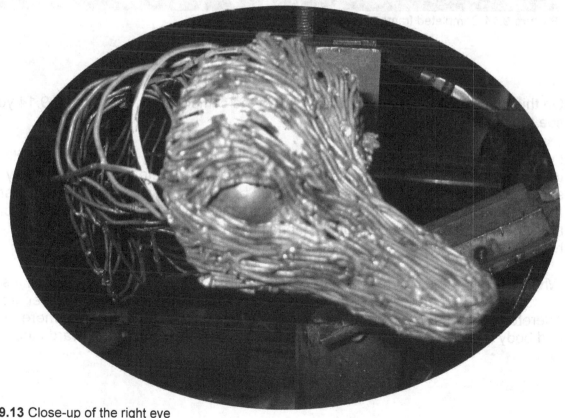

Picture 9.13 Close-up of the right eye with lashes and the finished nostrils.

Picture 9.14 Completed frame of the fox including legs and tail.

On this piece I want to see the framework of the complete body. In Picture 9.14 you can see the complete form.

I was going to fill in the tail first, since when filling in long hair, I need to start with the under- most layer of hair. On this piece I decided to complete the legs first. They are short-haired, just as the head is, and it would be advantageous to make them first. The tail hair will add extreme weight to the sculpture, just as it did with the head. To balance the sculpture, the rear section under the tail needs to be filled in first as it is short-haired.

When filling in the long hair, the under-most layer of hair has to be completed first. On the fox, the tip (or very end) of the tail is the under-most layer of hair on the entire body. Therefore, I start at the tip (end) of the tail and work my way up towards where the tail and body meet and then continue on up towards the neck and then towards the head.

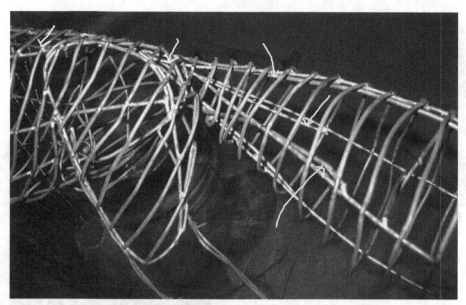

Picture 9.15 Arrows show the added bracing put in to give more strength where the tail attaches to the body.

When finished, this sculpture will be quite strong due to all the overlapping wire and all the welds. The beginning lines are very strong in themselves so I am choosing not to place additional bracing in the body.

In order to withstand all the moving around and different positions it will be put in, I now must add a specific area to provide strength that is needed in the tail and the legs. One will not be able to see through the finished piece; therefore, the inside bracing can easily be put in and does not need to follow the lines as suggested with the short haired animals. Another reason the bracing can be placed in now is that the shape is now correct. The legs will also be finished so that you cannot see through them, so it does not matter how the bracing is put into them.

I have used #11 soft steel wire for the outlines and hair lines. I chose this size of wire as it is large enough to be quite strong, yet small enough to make the detail I want. The bracing is 5/16" cold rolled steel rod. It is stronger than the wire. I could have used 1/4" soft steel rod.

Picture 9.16 Close-up of the rods installed to strengthen the front leg.(See the arrows.)

57

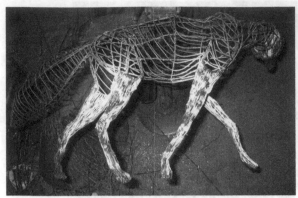

Picture 9.17 Right side of fox with legs filled in.

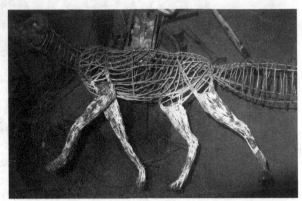

Picture 9.18 Left side of fox with legs filled in.

After putting in the bracing I fill in the legs, both inside and outside. Before I continue I want to see if the sculpture is well balanced when standing. At this point, if it does not stand, it will be easy to correct. I can also see if I like the motion.

In Picture 9.19 the arrow points to a handle-like addition that allows me to hold this sculpture in the vise. It will be removed as I get to that area to fill in with hair. By then, the sculpture will be heavy enough that I will no longer need the vise to hold the sculpture while pushing and pulling the wires into the shape needed.

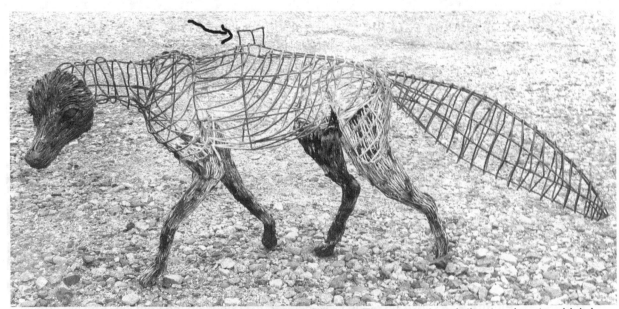

Picture 9.19 Left side of fox with head and legs filled in. The arrow is pointing to wires to which I attach the sculpture to the vise. They will be taken off when no longer needed.

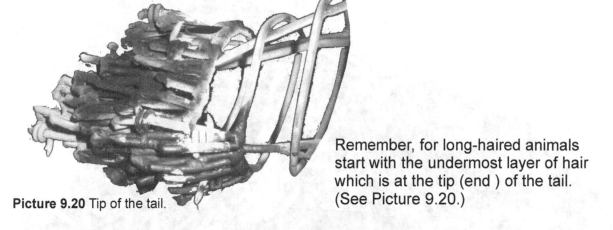
Picture 9.20 Tip of the tail.

Remember, for long-haired animals start with the undermost layer of hair which is at the tip (end) of the tail. (See Picture 9.20.)

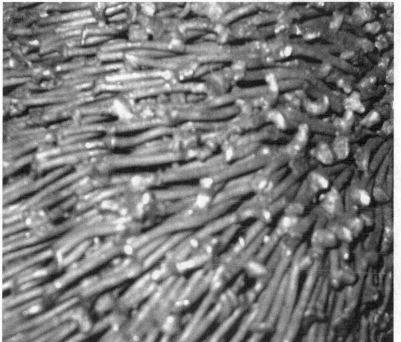

When welding the hair, make sure that you **do not make the lengths all the same.** The bracing you weld to is spaced evenly, but don't forget to make the lengths uneven to make it appear more natural. (See picture 9.21 and 9.22.)

Picture 9.21 Close-up of hair showing the wires are of different lengths.

Picture 9.22 The arrows point to the ends of the wire. These are different lengths.

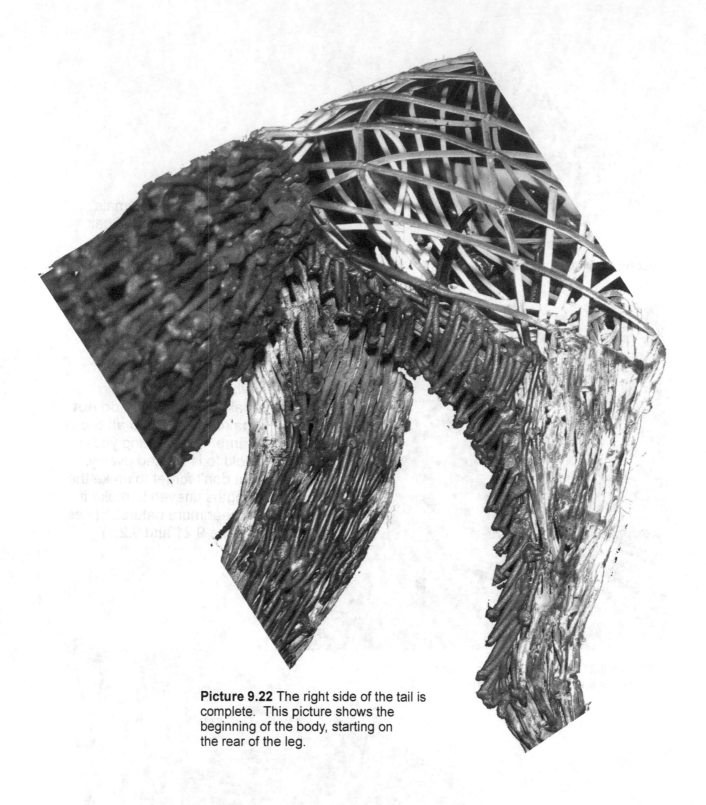

Picture 9.22 The right side of the tail is complete. This picture shows the beginning of the body, starting on the rear of the leg.

The tail is completed on the right side. The hair on the body can be started once the tail is completed (see Picture 9.22.). Again the undermost part must be filled first, so I am starting with the line that is at the end of the buttock and back of the leg. From there I can choose and continue to complete the side or finish the other side of the tail. I chose to fill in the side of this body before I completed the left side of the tail.

60

Next, I filled in the fringe on both sides of the rear legs. One side is completed first, then the other side. In Picture 9.23, I completed the fringe on the outside. Next, I filled the fringe on the inside. This required two to three lines of wire to make the fringe uneven, making it appear natural.

Picture 9.23 Arrow points to the fringe which shows from the other side.

The fringe in Picture 9.24 does not blend in well with the other leg hair. I will now blend that area (see Chapter 5 on blending) to make it appear more realistic.

Picture 9.25 shows the finished fringe area.

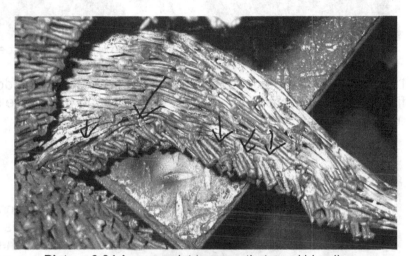

Picture 9.24 Arrows point to areas that need blending.

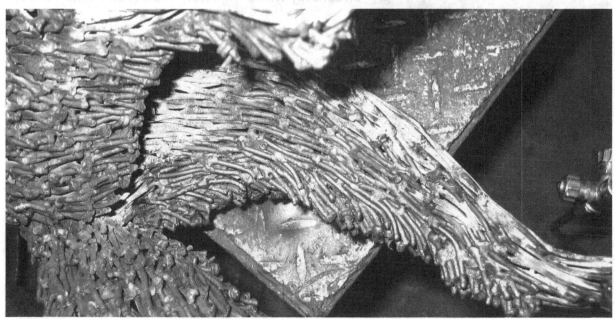

Picture 9.25 The blending of the fringe area is complete.

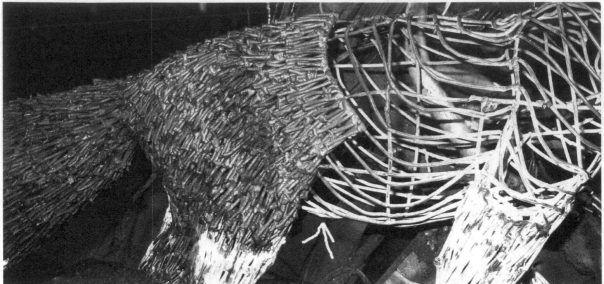

Picture 9.26 This is as far as I can go on the body until the underbelly (see arrow) has been filled in.

I have filled in as much of the side of the body as can be done until I have completed filling in the underbelly, because it underlies the hair of the side. In picture 9.26, the arrow indicates the area that needs to be filled first.

In Picture 9.27, you can see the area of the underbelly that needs to be filled. I started the fill along the center of the belly, from the rear to the chest. From there I filled up each side until the underbelly was completely filled (see Picture 9.28).

Picture 9.27 Beginning of the underbelly to the rear.

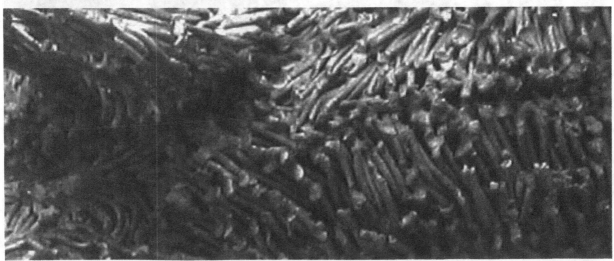

Picture 9.28 The underbelly is completed.

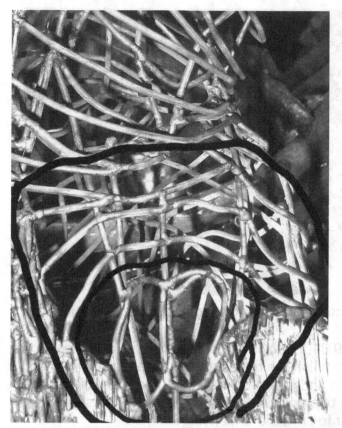

Picture 9.29 The outer circle is the complete chest; the inner circle shows the two circular areas to follow for the fill-in.

The hair for the chest area goes in different directions. Look carefully at the animal you are creating to make sure of the movement and the flow of the hair in all areas. For the chest area of this fox I used guidelines (see Picture 9.29, the upper part of the large circle) across the upper part of the chest and curved them up near the neck so they will blend in with the neck hair.

In Picture 9.29 the small circle shows two ovals, one on each side of the center line in which the hair goes around the oval. There are at least two lines of hair on each side. The oval line has hair going toward the outside on each side.

The center line will have hair going both to the left and right sides. See the finished product in Picture 9.30. The chest now gives the feeling of the hair of a fox.

Picture 9.30 The chest area is finished. See the movement of the hair.

Picture 9.31 The beginning of the belly on the right side.

As you can see in Pictures 9.29 through 9.31, I decided to complete the underside of the neck after completing the underbelly, then finish the right side. I chose to do this because I wanted to see a side completed and I was too impatient to do the left side of the tail before seeing the right side of the body completed. You can vary the sequence for doing the fill as long as you remember to fill in the underlying hair first.

Picture 9.31 shows the beginning of the fill of the belly on the right side. After completing the belly I stopped the right side at the neck, and then proceeded to the left side (see Picture 9.32). No particular reason. It just felt right to do it in this order, this time. I may do it in a different order another time.

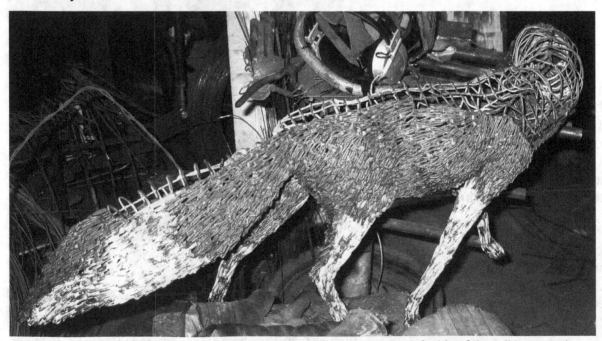

Picture 9.32 Right side is filled in up to the neck area and the left side of the tail is started.

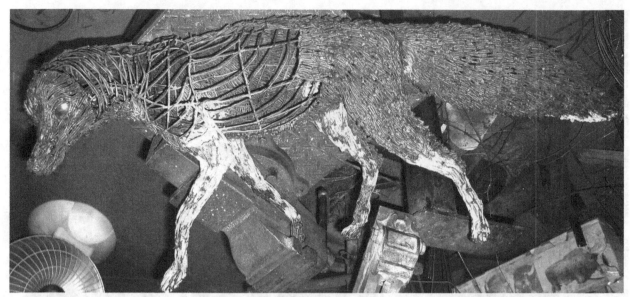

Picture 9.33 The tail is complete. Now I will fill in the left side of the body.

Often I complete the entire tail first. This time, I did the tail on the right side only, and decided to complete the right side of the body before completing the tail. I now proceed to the left side. Picture 9.33 shows the tail completed as well as the beginning of the left side. Picture 9.34 shows the left side of the body completed.

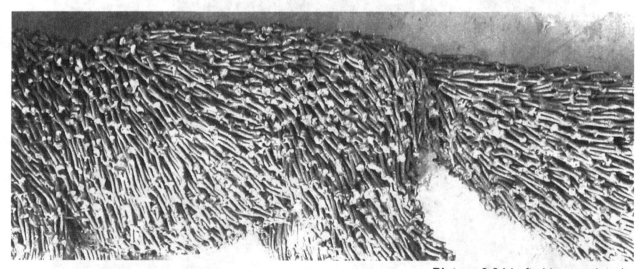

Picture 9.34 Left side completed.

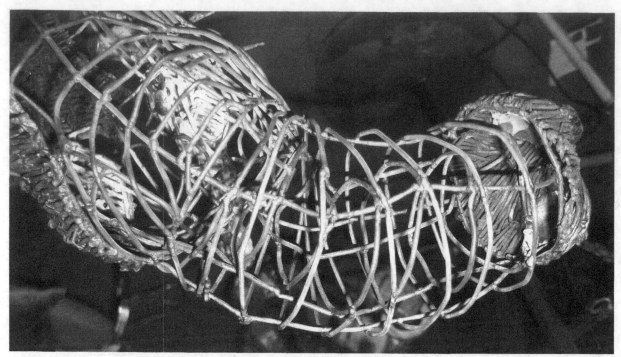

Picture 9.35 Additional guidelines are added to the neck.

The original lines I made for the neck were not big enough so I have made larger circles outside them to enlarge the finished neck. (See Pictures 9.35 and 9.36.)

If this were not a long-haired animal, it would be important to remove the original lines; they would show in a finished short-haired or hairless animal. In the long-haired animal these first lines will not show in the finished product.

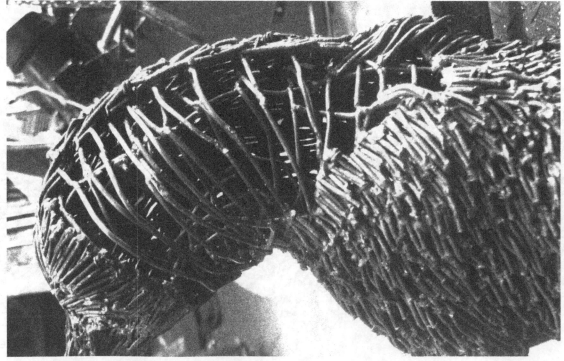

Picture 9.36 The left side of the neck needs to be filled in.

66

Picture 9.37 Top of the completed sculpture. The area the arrow points to is not correct.

Picture 9.38 Bottom of the completed sculpture. It looks good.

Pictures 9.37 and 9.38 are pictures of the top and bottom of the finished sculpture. After studying it I see several areas are not correct. The top (See Picture 9.37) shows the right hip and belly are not large enough (see arrow). There is more explanation on the following page. The bottom of the fox looks pretty good. (See Picture 9.38.) The owner has named this piece *"The Fox."*

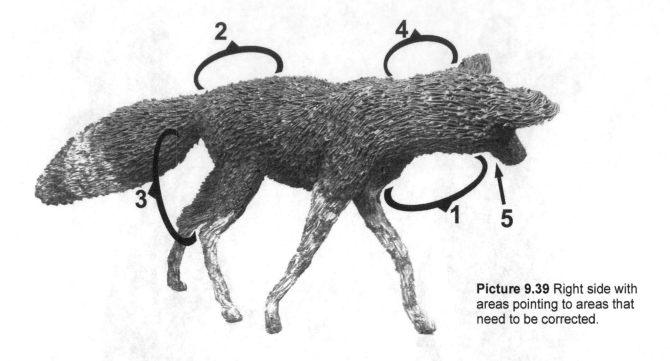

Picture 9.39 Right side with areas pointing to areas that need to be corrected.

The following corrections need to be made on both sides of the fox:
1. The chest will have to be moved further forward and the bottom of the neck enlarged.
2. The top of the buttocks will have to be enlarged.
3. The rear legs and the rear of the butt need to be made larger toward the back.
4. The top of the neck and shoulder areas need to be larger.
5. I will add tufts to each side of the cheeks.

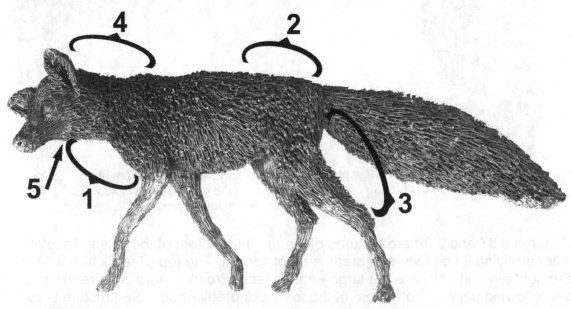

Picture 9.40 Left side with arrows pointing to areas out that need to be corrected.

68

Chapter 10 - Corrections on the Fox

What a disappointment to have to correct these areas, especially when I thought the Fox was completed. I was anxious to get this done, too! It must be corrected as I am proud of my work and I want all my creations to be the best that I can make, regardless of the time it takes. I rework what needs to be corrected. **It is always worth it!** "A job worth doing is worth doing right."

I have several different ways to approach each correction:

1. Cut out the area completely and re-weld the cut-out area as if it were the first time.

2. Weld over the incorrect area without cutting it out. I can do this on a long-haired critter but not when correcting a short-haired or hairless animal. On a long-haired animal you would not see the incorrect area when it is completed.

3. Cut out the bad area. Then take the cut-out part and reshape, if necessary. place this cut-out piece back into the hole and weld it back on. This cut-out piece often does not fit back in the hole exactly, so the areas that are left open are then filled in and blended.

The first correction is shown in Picture 10.1, which is the rear area on the left side of the fox. I used the third approach, described above to correct this area.

I have a plasma cutter and this is what I used to cut out the bad area. If you do not have a plasma cutter, you can cut it out with the oxygen-acetylene cutting torch.

Once it was removed, I shaped the cut-out piece and the edges of the main piece, then fit the piece back into the correct position.

Picture 10.1 Shows the hole that was left after cutting out the area that needed to be corrected on the left rear leg and buttocks.

Pictures 10.2 and 10.3 are front and rear views of the piece that was cut out of the left hindquarter and rear leg. There was a fairly big space left all around the cutout piece.

I placed guidelines in the open spaces to help with the fill-in.

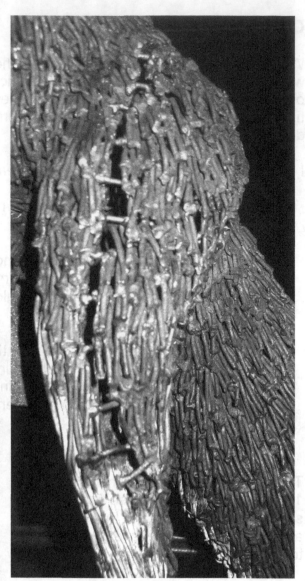

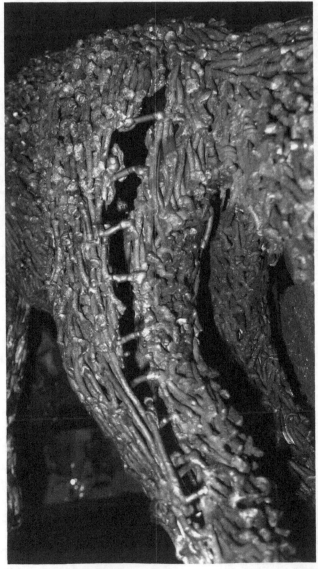

Picture 10.2 When the cut-out piece was replaced, there was a lot of open space left. I put guidelines in to help fill in that area. This picture shows the front part of the replaced piece.

Picture 10.3 This picture shows the rear part of the replaced cut-out area and the guidelines I put in to help fill in that area.

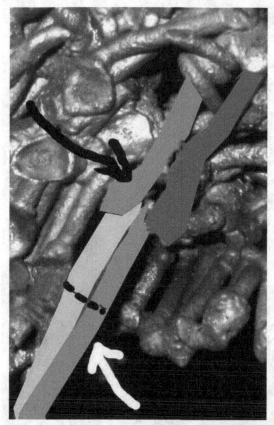

Previously I welded the hair by overlapping the previous layer. When correcting these areas there will be some places where I cannot overlap as the top layer is already there.

When this happens I weld the wire under the top layer. Picture 10.4 shows the strand of wire (the lighter grey wires indicated by the white arrow) that I welded under the upper wire (the darker grey wires indicated by the black arrow). I do it this way when the top must overlap the part I am currently welding.

I weld the wire as I did on this piece. (See the dotted line in Picture 10.4 on the lighter grey wires.)

Picture 10.5 shows the finished weld and cut wires.

Picture 10.4 Illustration of welding under a wire.

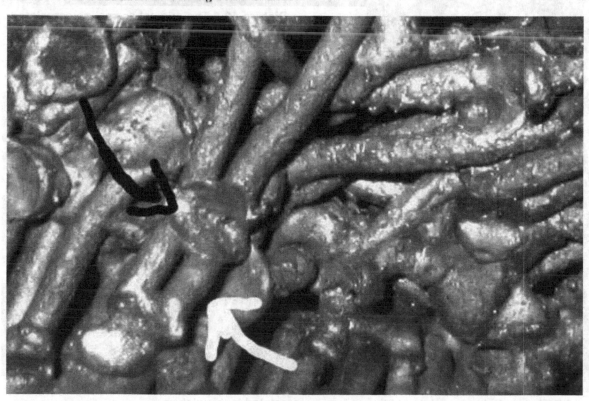

Picture 10.5 The black arrow points to where I welded the wire under the top wire. The white arrow points to where I cut that wire off with the torch as I welded it.

71

Picture 10.6 shows the completed correction. However, after looking at it I see that some areas need to be blended more.

The circled area in Picture 10.7 needed to be blended more.

In Picture 10.8, additional blending is complete.

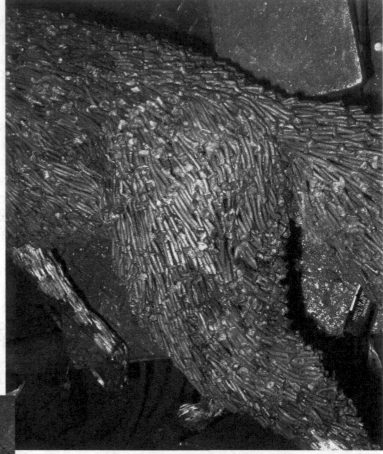

Picture 10.6 The original correction completed.

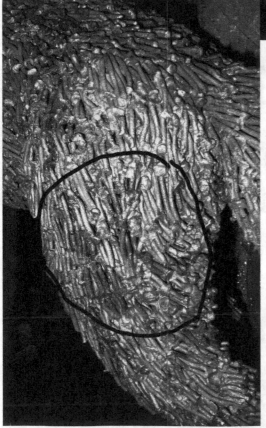

Picture 10.7 The circled area points out the area that still needs to be blended.

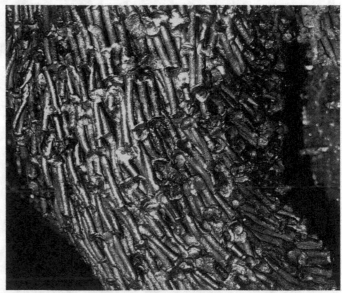

Picture 10.8 The area that needed to be blended is completed in this picture.

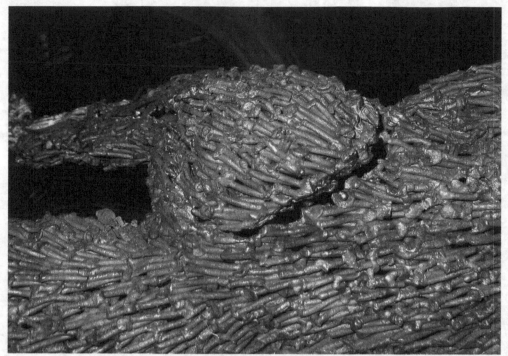

Picture 10.9 A hole is also left on the top of the left hip after replacing the cut-out piece.

The top of the same area (left rear hip) also had a hole to be filled when the cut-out piece was replaced. Picture 10.9 shows this area before the fill-in. Picture 10.10 shows an area that still needs to be blended after the fill=in. Can you identify that out area?

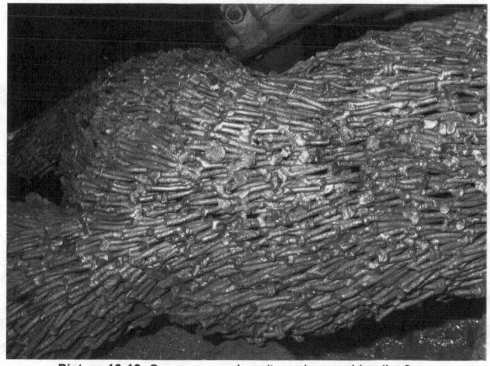

Picture 10.10 Can you see where it needs more blending?

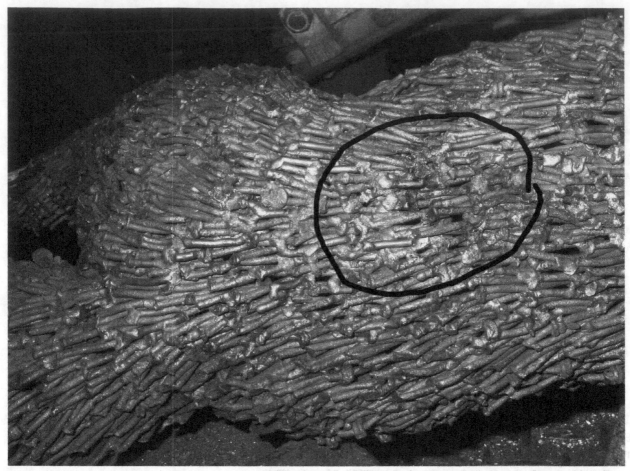

Picture 10.11 The circled area is in need of more blending.

In Picture 10.11, the circled area is the part that needs more work. Picture 10.12 shows the blending completed.

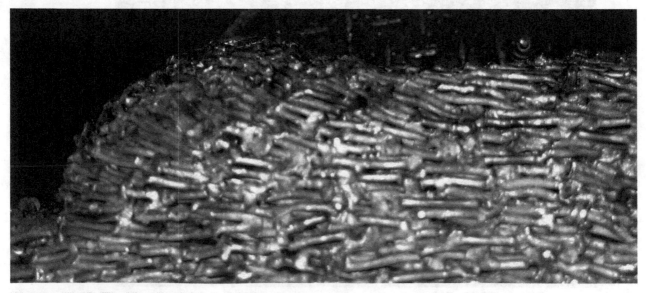

Picture 10.12 The blending is completed.

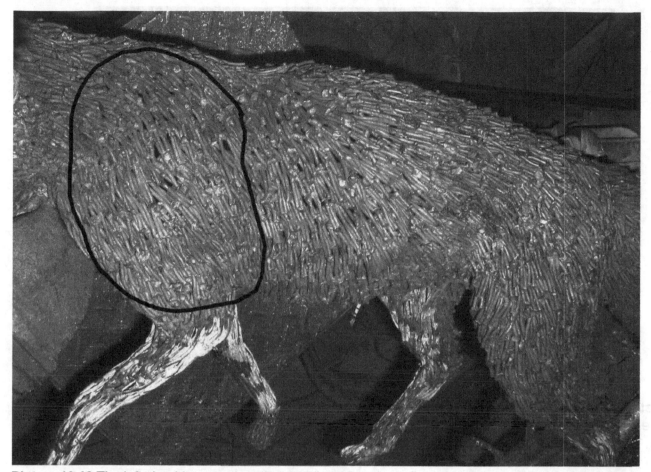

Picture 10.13 The left shoulder area (see the circle) needs to be enlarged.

Next, I corrected the left shoulder. In Picture 10.13, the circle shows the area that needed to be built up.

I used approach #2 (welding over) to correct this area. It is large enough to use approach #3 (cutting out and reshaping), but the cut out-out area would not blend in very well. Approach #1 (cutting out and welding the area all over again) would not work to my advantage. Since this is a long-haired animal and I will not see this part after it is corrected, I do not need to take the time to cut it out. I used approach #2 and placed the new guidelines over the area that needed correction. (See Picture 10.14.) If this were a short-haired or hairless animal, I would have had to use approach #1.

To start, I placed the guidelines and then filled in the hair.

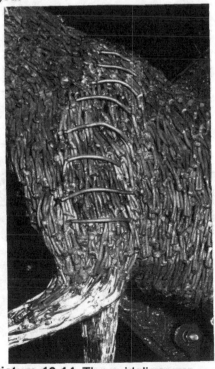

Picture 10.14 The guidelines are placed over the area to be raised.

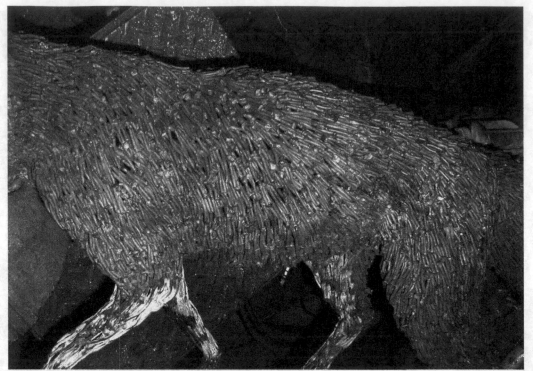
Picture 10.15 The completed shoulder and rear areas of the left side.

Picture 10.15 shows the corrected shoulder and the rear areas on the left side. Next, you see the corrections I made on the right side of *"The Fox,"* using approach #2. Picture 10.16 shows the guidelines used to correct areas on the right side, including the neck.

Picture 10.16 The right side had many areas that needed to be enlarged. This picture shows the guidelines I used to correct this side.

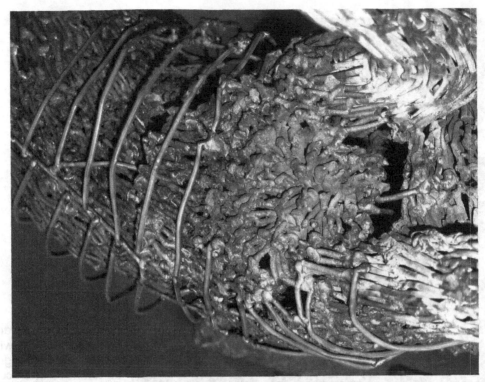

Picture 10.17 Shows guidelines for bottom of the neck and lifted chest area.

I found that with the enlargement of the neck, the chest had to be moved towards the front and lowered to fit the flow of the neck. Picture 10.17 shows the under part of the neck with the guidelines for the neck. You can see a little of the right shoulder guidelines as well. The chest was moved to match the neck.

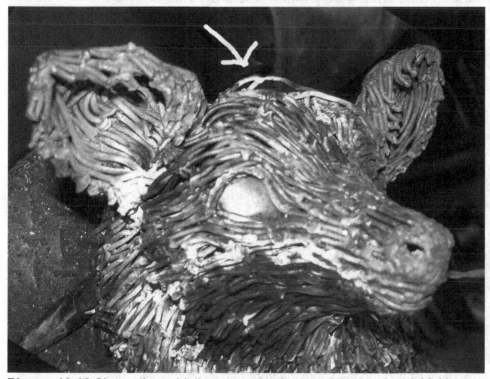

Another area that needed correction is the top of the head. This had to be built up a bit higher. See the arrow in Picture 10.18 that points to the guidelines I followed to heighten the top of the head.

Picture 10.18 Shows the guidelines to make the top of the head a bit higher.

77

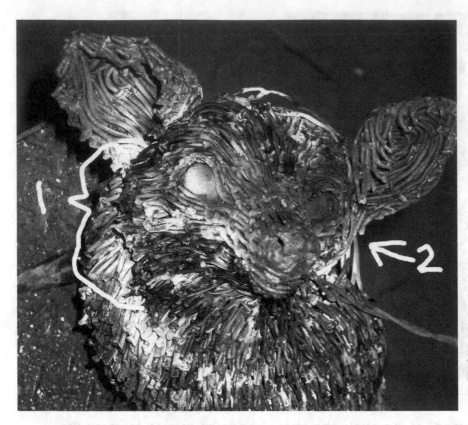

Picture 10.19 #1 and #2 point to the areas where the fox has tufts of longer hair. I do not have them completed in this picture.

I forgot the tufts of long hair that are on the side of a fox's face. In Picture 10.19, arrows #1 and #2 point to where these tufts should be placed. Picture 10.20 shows the completed tufts.

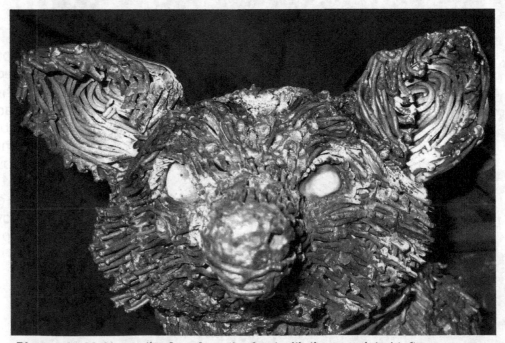

Picture 10.20 Shows the face from the front with the completed tufts.

I finished all of the corrections I thought needed to be made. I looked at the "finished" product and found that **many things were still out of proportion!** I took a picture; unfortunately, the picture did not turn out, so I do not have a picture to show you the many areas that needed work. This time the answer to "How long does it take?" is " A really long time" since I didn't get it correct the first time, and in some of the areas it was not correct until the second or third time.

Picture 10.21 The back is raised. Arrows #1 points to the open areas left by lifting the back. #2 is the beginning of the cut that will allow the belly to be lowered. #3 points to where the area above the tail needs to be raised and blended with the raised back.

So begins what I truly hope are the last changes; these changes are pretty major! First, the top of the back needs to be raised, then the belly lowered.

In Picture 10.21, Arrow #1 shows the space where the back was cut completely off and raised up about 1 inch at the shoulder side and about 1- 1 ½ inches in the tail area.

Arrow #2 points to one of the cuts needed to lower the belly area.

Arrow #3 shows where the tail meets the back. This must be filled in to create a nice curve where it meets the tail.

Picture 10.22 shows the space created on the left side when the back was lifted. This picture also shows guidelines I used to fill in that space.

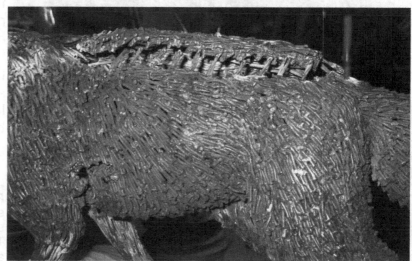

Picture 10.22 Shows the space left when the back was raised, and the guidelines used to attach the raised back to the left side.

Picture 10.23 When the belly was lowered, a large hole resulted on the left side. This picture shows the hole and the guidelines that will be used to fill in the hole.

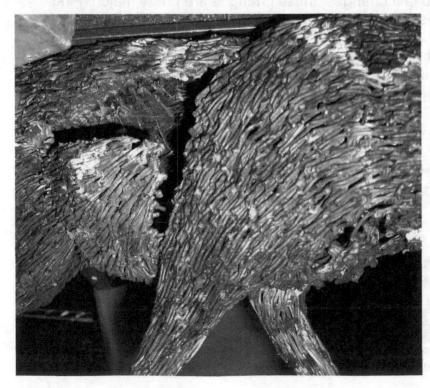

The chest and the belly had to be lowered in order to transition into the enlarged neck. The neck was enlarged to match the head.

Pictures 10.23 and 10.24 show the holes that were left when the chest and belly were lowered.

Picture 10.24 shows the open space that resulted on the right side when the belly was lowered. The chest also had to be lowered a third time to match the neck and the belly.

Picture 10.25 The neck was too large on the left side and needed to be cut out and redone.

The neck area was too thick and had to be cut out and slimmed. (See Pictures 10.25 and 10.26.)

The back and belly have been completed and I actually like them!

Picture 10.26 View from the underside of the correction on the neck.

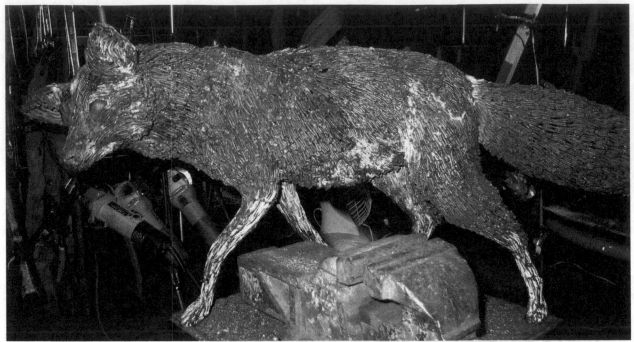

Picture 10.27 All the corrections are filled in and blended.

Picture 10.29 is of what I hoped was the finished sculpture. It is time to check all over the fox and make sure all the wires are firmly welded and that all the blending that may be needed is completed. Then, I take pictures from all angles and set the sculpture in a place that I will walk by or see often throughout the day. When looking at pictures of a piece, I will see an incorrect area that I may not see by just looking at the sculpture. It is also imperative that I take several days to study the finished piece, seeing it off and on, to be able to be sure that everything is correct.

After studying this piece for several days and looking at the pictures, I find there is something that I do not like. The neck is too high in one area. (See arrow in Picture 10.28.) I heated it, beat it down with a large hammer and then re-welded some wires that came loose when I hammered it on it.

Picture 10.28 The arrow points to one area that still needs work.

Here he is, complete and the color of a fox.
The extra time invested paid off handsomely!

How long does it take? As long as needed to get everything correct. *"Pegasus"* went together really well with very few alterations. This one took 2 ½ times longer than I would have expected. I feel it was worth it as I like the finished sculpture far more than before all the corrections.

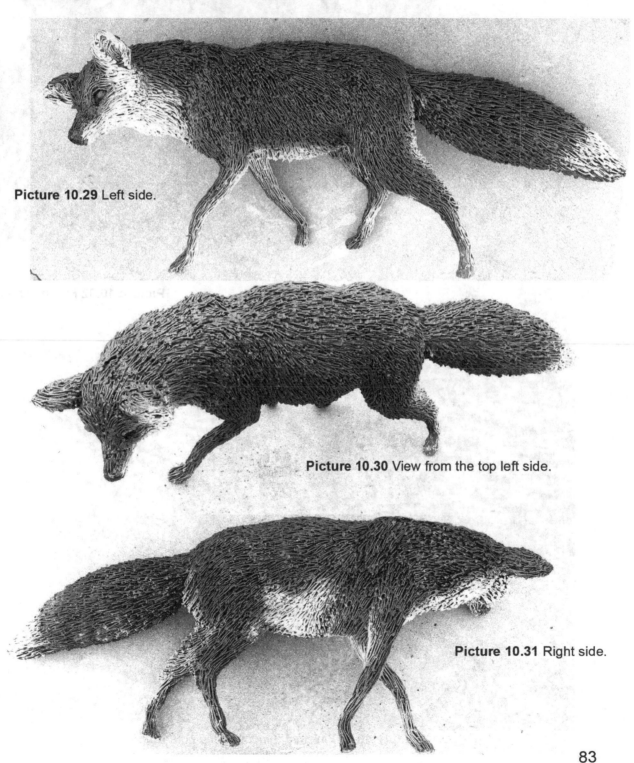

Picture 10.29 Left side.

Picture 10.30 View from the top left side.

Picture 10.31 Right side.

Closeups of the head of the finished sculpture.

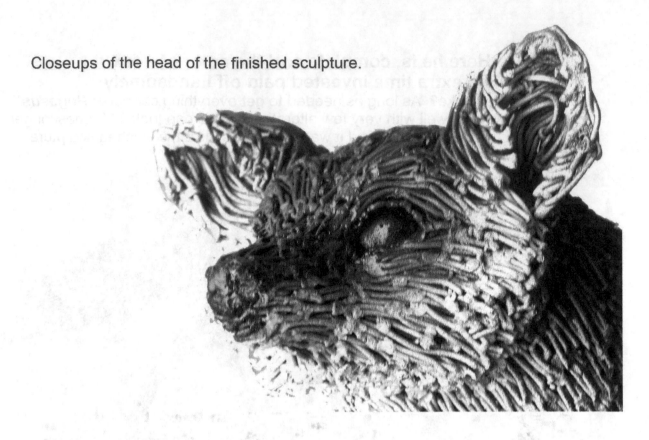

Picture 10.32 Finished head.

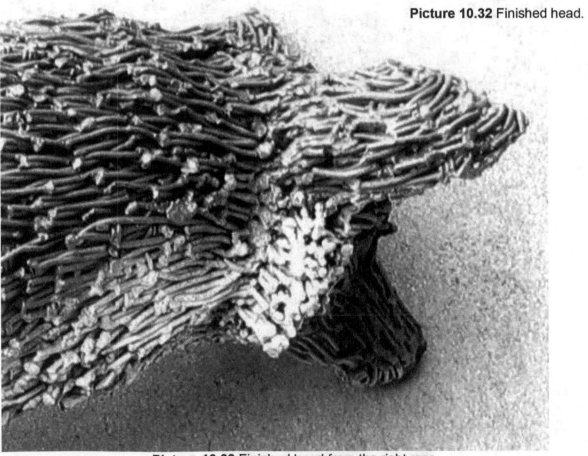

Picture 10.33 Finished head from the right rear.

Part VI
Other Long-Haired/Wool/Fur Animals

Chapter 11

Creating a Llama

Again, when creating long-hair/wool/fur on animals, following the lines is not as crucial. The shape is most important as well as the flow of the long hair/wool/fur. Start by making the shape of the outer form. Make lines for the hair/wool/fur all around about 1 ½ inches apart as you do for a bird's wing. Picture 11.1 shows the complete beginning frame

Picture 11.2 The head of the llama is completed with the beginning lines to add the fur to the neck.

Picture 11.1 Beginning frame for a sculpture of a llama with reinforcement. (See the dark lines.)

This is a life-sized llama. I started with the head, making it like a short-haired animal, as the llama's head has short wool. Then I made the legs as they are also short wool. Next was the basic framework of a llama, attaching the head and legs to the body. When I am sure that the shape is correct, I put lots of reinforcement inside so it is strong. The dark areas in Pictures 11.1 are the reinforcement in this piece. Then I made a framework of lines all around the neck to which I welded one wire at a time side by side to each of the lines to create the look of wool. (See Picture 11.2.)

Picture 11.3 shows that I started with the legs and worked my way up to the body as the leg wool lies under the body wool. Again, I also made sure the texture looks like llama wool.

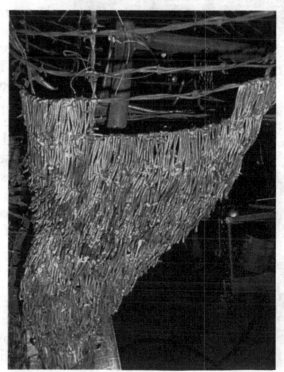

Picture 11.3 Begin the filling with the legs. Be sure the texture looks like wool.

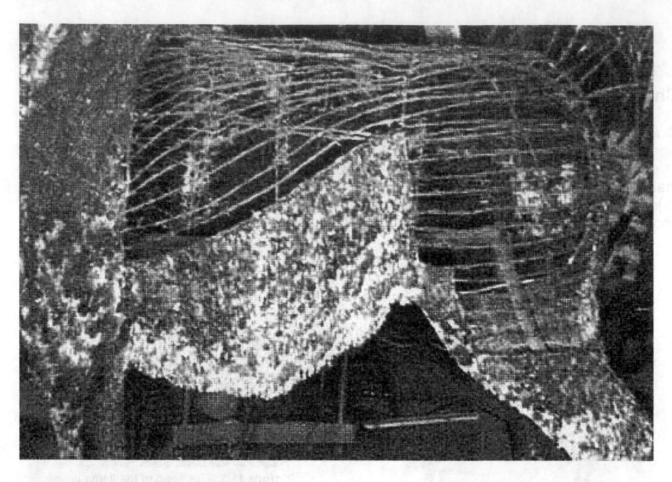

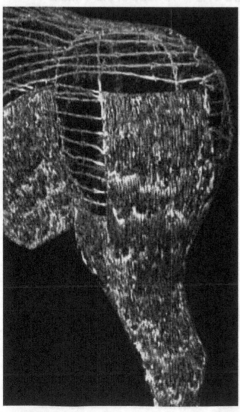

Here are a few pictures of the fill in process for the llama. It is good to sort of follow the line shapes I talked about in the section on lines. You can see that I followed the flow of the belly in the picture above.

The pictures to the right and left show some of the fill in

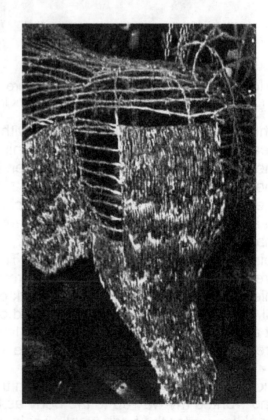

Here is the completed sculpture of the llama pictured with a live llama.
(Note that my llama is better behaved and eisier to care for.)

Picture 11.7 Sculpted *"Felipe"*, with live llama named Cince' de Mayo
made of barbed wire then powder-coated with painted highlights

Coyote

The llama has fur; a coyote has long hair. I began the
coyote a bit differently than I did the fox. I started with
the basic frame and then filled in, creating the head later.
As I have said before, you can pick the order for the
fill-in, as long as you put in the under-lying hair, first.

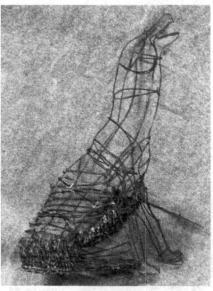

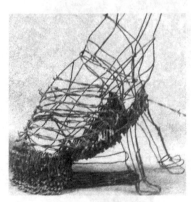

Picture 11.9 shows the
beginning fill-in of the coyote.
I started at the butt and rear
legs, because that is the
bottom-most area, so the
sculpture is stable while I
work on it. Picture 11.9
shows the complete
beginning frame for the
Coyote.

Picture 11.8 The beginning
frame for a coyote.

Picture 11.9 Complete beginning
frame for a coyote.

Picture 11.10 is the finished coyote and it is the mascot for Cadawalder Middle School in Las Vegas, Nevada.

Elk

Another animal that is a combination of short hair and long hair is an elk. The body is mostly short hair with areas of long hair under the chin, neck and belly.

Pictures 11.11 shows a finished elk head that is a mount for above a fireplace. Picture 11.12 shows a closeup of the long hair under the neck.

Picture 11.10 *"Hungry for Knowledge ... Howling for Success"* Made of barbed wire, powder-coated and painted for color.

Picture 11.12 Close-up of the long hair on the neck..

Picture 11.11 Elk Head Mount for above a fireplace.

Part VII
The Finishing Process

Chapter 12- Finishes and Coloring a Barbed Wire Sculpture

Sandblasting

To clean the pieces up after welding, I recommend sandblasting because it takes them down to the clean metal. From here you can color it in many different ways.

If you do not sandblast, the surface will color differently in some areas, depending on the kind of finish the metal has. Areas that have been ground or welded will often rust faster and have different colors if not sandblasted.

Wire Brushing

Wire brushing will polish the surface and can clean up the rust and dirt; however, with barbed wire it is hard to get to all the areas due to the twist of the wire. I think it works better if you have the piece sandblasted first. Then polish with the wire brush. It will rust after a time unless you spray it with a clear lacquer or acrylic. When spraying, remember that the piece will get a bit darker in color.

Rusting.

If you want a rusted finish fast, sandblast first, spray with vinegar and then wash the vinegar off with water. As it dries, a nice surface rust color will appear. If this is a table top piece I would then spray it with a clear lacquer or acrylic. The color will stay this way. Alternately, you can leave it and the color will usually darken as it ages.

Again, rusting will be more even if the piece is sandblasted to clean it.

Powder-coating

You can take the piece to a company that will powder-coat. If they can powder-coat one color only, I have them powder-coat it with the predominant color of the finished piece. I then use a high quality paint (such as automobile paint) to make the highlights or other colors. This will last pretty well. However, as always, due to the twist of the wire it will be hard to get it all covered.

Dye and Metal Coatings

You can find various colors in dye that are specific for steel at *Sculpt Nouveau* http://www.sculpt.com/catalog_98/patina/rypatinas.htm and follow their instructions.

There are probably many other ways to color a piece just use your imagination and experiment..

Have a terrific time Creating.

Please send me pictures of what you have done.

*If I can help you in any way, check out my
web page at www.sculptures-by-bjh.com
or contact me at bjh@sculptures-by-bjh.com.
You can call me at (208) 887-9632*

Best Wishes

Bernie Jestrabek-Hart

Bernie Jestrabek-Hart